# A COLLECTOR'S GUIDE TO

# 20TH-CENTURY
# TOYS

# A COLLECTOR'S GUIDE TO
# 20TH-CENTURY
# TOYS

Consultant Editor: JAMES OPIE
with
DUNCAN CHILCOTT  JULIA HARRIS

THE WELLFLEET PRESS

A COLLECTOR'S GUIDE TO 20TH-CENTURY TOYS

First published in 1990 by Wellfleet Books
a division of Book Sales Inc.
110 Enterprise Avenue
Secaucus, New Jersey 07094

This book was edited and designed by Anness Law Limited
4a The Old Forge, 7 Caledonian Road, London N1 9DX

ISBN 1-55521-544-0

Printed and bound in Czechoslovakia

Photographs are reprinted courtesy of Phillips London (pages 7, 8, 9, 12, 13, 14, 15, 18, 20, 21, 22, 23, 27, 35, 36, 43, 45, 47, 58, 59, 60, 61, 62, 64, 65, 67, 68, 69, 70, 71, 72, 73, 74, 75, 76, 77, 84, 85, 89, 90, 91), Bonhams London (pages 13, 31, 32, 33, 34, 35, 36, 37, 38, 49, 50, 51, 52, 53, 54, 55, 56, 57, 78, 79, 80, 81, 92), Christies London (pages 10, 24, 25, 30, 38, 39, 40, 41, 44, 45, 88), Sothebys London (pages 19, 20, 45, 46), Mattel (page 15), New Cavendish Books (pages 63, 65), Palitoy (page 82), Corgi (page 82), Ertl (page 83).

# CONTENTS

# INTRODUCTION

*The collecting of toys has become fashionable,*

*as opposed to eccentric, since the 1950s. The*

*squirrel instinct is strong in all of us. Collect-*

*ing is fun, whether the impulse is the intellec-*

*tual discipline of forming well-researched,*

*coherent and complete assemblies, or just to be a*

*magpie and acquire a selection of interesting things.*

Toys provide a froth of fun for the whole family—they can be diverting and entertaining, educating and amusing. It is no wonder, therefore, that so many adults have chosen to continue the collecting instincts of their younger years. Nor is it strange that ladies usually collect dolls and men collect toy soldiers. The emotions that can be rekindled by collecting are basic and satisfying, allowing us, for instance, to acquire the equivalent of the toy that we envied many years ago in a shop window or in the possession of a friend.

Today, looking back, some of the personalities of recent times were evidently fascinated by toys. Winston Churchill and Robert Louis Stevenson wrote about their toy soldiers; Queen Victoria's collection of dolls was legendary; H. G. Wells wrote two whole books on the virtues of floor games and little wars; and Malcolm Forbes and Douglas Fairbanks Jr. have been numbered among the ranks of toy soldier collectors. As the supreme accolade of the 1974 Empire Exhibition to Queen Mary, it was decided to construct a supreme doll's house, which contained toy everything—including toy toys!

This book introduces the beauty and enchantment of the most collectable toys of the twentieth century. In a short outline of the toy industry, it will become clear why the most widely collected toys are those of the last hundred years. The contributors to this book are all authorities in their various fields; since most collectors confine themselves to relatively narrow sub-

jects, the opportunity provided by this book to explore the relationships between, for instance, dolls and toy soldiers, is fresh and interesting. With such a fascinating subject as toys there is something new to learn even from relatively short discussions.

It is said by collectors who join together to swap, buy, sell and research their toys that they do it for fun, instruction and profit, in that order. Although an untutored investor would not think of investing in toys purely in anticipation of a rise in prices, the expectation that prices will rise leads many collectors to put money into their collections, feeling that if they ever leave collecting, they might get more than their money back.

### THE TOYMAKING REVOLUTION
Playing is probably the most important part of growing up. Learning has traditionally been a serious discipline, to teach young minds to concentrate on the unwelcome necessities of life. Play, by contrast, is the free expression of the increasing intellect, the joyous experience of becoming more able to control one's surroundings that children at first find so daunting and frustrating.

Toys are the tools of play, and anything that is

Right: *Childhood memories of Christmases and the temptations of toy-shop windows instill the adult world of the serious toy collector with an enthusiasm and passion found in few other areas.*

Above: *An attractive group reflecting the range of major popular collectable subjects covered by this volume.*

pressed into play's service becomes a toy. For most of history the majority of toys have been home-made. Wood, clay and lead were the earliest toymaking materials for cottage industries, while jewellers and goldsmiths made toys for the very rich. Soon after each inventive advance in the industrial revolution, however, mass production was harnessed to provide toys at consumable prices. Means of mass distribution were also in place by the beginning of the twentieth century, and there is very little that today's marketing executive could do in principle to improve on a 1900 Sears Roebuck catalogue.

There has been much change in the course of the twentieth century. In 1913 the department store Gamages of Holborn, in England, was a cornucopia of toys culled by the industrious proprietor from the four corners of the earth. The Gamages Grand Xmas Bazaar catalogue (a huge amount of business was done by post) devoted 156 pages to toys: trains (25 pages), steam-powered toys (9 pages), modelling (13 pages), wireless sets (16 pages), chemistry sets (3 pages), boats (14 pages), aeroplanes (6 pages), tin toys (11 pages), toy soldiers (6 pages), play outfits (5 pages), musical toys (3 pages), kindergarten toys—cut-out, painting, weaving, and beadwork (7 pages), constructional toys (7 pages), toy theatres (1 page), Steiff soft toys (4 pages), animals (2 pages), doll's houses, dolls and accessories (12 pages), and ride-on toys (12 pages).

Of items that are collectable today, dolls are much in evidence—though whereas Steiff toys are included there is not a single teddy bear—tinplate toys are present in various categories, toy trains are in plentiful supply, and toy soldiers are listed in full from the William Britains' range of the time, with some German imports as well; die-cast toys have not yet been introduced, the equivalent toys all being of tin or cast iron, and media toys have not yet arrived.

The traditional fount of all toys at this time was Germany, but in Britain, William Britains was well established, and Frank Hornby had recently started marketing Meccano. World War I effectively ended German dominance in the toy export trade.

Looking at an equivalent Christmas catalogue today, that of the Argos Showrooms in England, what do we find? The overall impression is that everything is made in plastic rather than metal, wood or paper. The 37 pages are devoted to die-cast cars and racetrack (3 pages), musical toys (1 page), kindergarten toys (4 pages), Lego constructional toys (3 pages), soft toys (1 page), doll's houses, dolls and accessories (8 pages), ride-on toys (4 pages), action character toys such as He-man, Transformers, Action Force and Ghostbusters (5 pages), and baby toys (8 pages).

In spite of the nearly 80-year time difference, the overall themes are still the same. Dolls have been given brand names such as Barbie or Sindy. Tin toys have been replaced by die-cast or plastic. Toy trains have disappeared, banished to a more specialized model market. Toy soldiers have become spacemen or superheroes. The major differences are firstly in the materials and making of the toys themselves, and secondly in the influence of mass media, particularly television.

Plastic has become the preferred material for dollmakers (replacing bisque and composition), for toy soldiers, animals and figures (replacing lead, wood and composition), and for cheap and ephemeral amusements (replacing paper or card). Even in the area of soft toys, soft plastic has made an impact, although here the traditional filled fabric still reigns. The most popular constructional toy of the last two generations, Lego, has taken over the role performed in the first half of the century by Meccano. Perhaps the biggest impact of plastic has been in the category of toys for very young children, where beautifully shaped and coloured toys are now safe to suck, because even when the toys are painted, the paint is based on plastic instead of lead.

One recurrent theme in the progress of toymaking is the search for realism in toys. To make a true model of something takes a great deal more time and trouble than to make an approximation, and therefore the quality of miniature toys is often judged by how true

Below: *Noah's Ark. A typical wooden Noah's Ark, c.1990, complete with a vast range of pairs of animals carved from wood. Lead figures of zoo animals only became popular in the 1930s. Until then, these beautiful biblical sets were the most popular way of depicting the world's wild animals. Phillips London.*

*Above: A group of very fine toys from a sale at Christie's Glasgow, in 1986. The two teddy bears are by Steiff, and the locomotive is a Bing.*

to life they are. The advent of plastic made it so much simpler to produce realistic-looking models of things, that plastic model kits became a whole new area of the toy industry from the 1940s onwards. Yet plastic realism is appearance only, and a die-cast metal car feels more like a car than its plastic equivalent. However, plastic allied to die-casting, applied to the production of toy vehicles, has now made possible a feast of realism and play value at absurdly low prices.

## THE IMPACT OF TELEVISION
Television has been the other innovation that has changed the face of the toy industry. Since it has been possible to advertize toys on television, the best toys have reached their marketplace with almost magical efficiency, reinforcing the propensity of children to catch on to the latest craze. Television also provides the most pervasive opportunities to sell toys linked to characters appearing 'on the box', known as character merchandize. So fascinating and famous are these

products that they have rapidly become some of the most sought-after of all collectable toys.

Advertizing on television, buying licences to sell character merchandize and then manufacturing plastic and die-cast toys in the quantities necessary to profit on the transactions takes capital. The toy industry is notorious for products that do well one year and badly the next, and so now includes a small number of large international companies, some doing well and others badly, along with a host of young underfunded hopefuls.

## THE WORLD SCENE
The list of famous trademarks and companies, some once boasting to be the world's largest toymakers, that have now been taken over or liquidated includes Meccano, Louis Marx, Lines Brothers, Lesney, Fisher-Price, Mettoy and Britains. Others, such as Marklin, Lehmann, Solido, Mattel, Lego and Kenner-Parker continue an independent tradition as toymakers, many both sourcing and selling their products throughout the world. Toymaking is one of the most international of all trades, and potentially one of the foremost foreign currency earners for developing countries.

Above: *A good way for the new collector to gain experience is to attend auction viewings, where toys of all types can be seen and actually handled with the assistance of attendant experts.*

Right: *A very handsome pair of soldiers, one mounted, and one on foot blowing a bugle.*

Since collectors most naturally collect the toys they were brought up with, in each country it is the native products of that country which are most collected, often to the total exclusion of foreigners. This book introduces the international possibilities of toy collecting to hitherto national collectors, to mirror the evolution of the toy industry itself.

### TOY COLLECTING AS A HOBBY

Apart from their visual appeal and nostalgic satisfaction, toys as an adult collection have much to commend them. Miniature people and objects have always held a fascination for children that is still exerted upon grown-ups. The majority of toys, and all of our collectable themes, fall into this area. The various portrayals of real or fictitious life mirror the concerns, interests and imagination of our immediate forbears, in a way that little else can manage.

A good collection can be fitted into a reasonably small space. A car collector can, for instance, easily fit five hundred cars into his garage! Toys are small, easily handled and easily stored. Actually playing with the toys and having the collection accessible adds much to the enjoyment of them, and is so much better than looking at them in a museum.

To understand how all these toys originated, who dreamed them up, their purpose, commercial and idealistic, and their success in the marketplace, needs a great deal of research. The collecting of catalogues and researching of trade magazines and directories is fascinating for the toy enthusiast. All toymakers have

Above: *Wargame for James Bond. Another example of toys for adults, this wargaming layout is famous for featuring in the James Bond film 'The Living Daylights'.*

been searching for the more amusing and attractive toy with which to make their fortune . . . the better their success, the more collectable it is likely to be today, although some of the grotesque failures can also be interesting by contrast.

Toys are an art form in that they have to appeal to adults and children, they have to be safe and they have to be made for a price that will sell. Some toy-makers have departed from realism into designs that were too cute, cheap, comic or fantastic. Conversely, sometimes they have been so sophisticated that children could not appreciate them, or so gruesome that adults could not tolerate them.

Children tend to appreciate quantity rather than quality, and so pocket-money toys bought from the corner shop tend to be poor but plentiful. The big stores will contain the quality merchandize bought by the parent for Christmas or birthdays. The successful toy, in the end, is one that will actually amuse, and be seen to amuse, the child.

Earlier in the century, boys appeared to need more toys than girls, perhaps because girls were encouraged to be interested in domestic and adult affairs at an earlier age than boys. In the toy catalogues mentioned previously, the 1913 one contained 92 pages of boys' toys and only 19 pages of girls' toys, together with 45 pages of toys that might do for either. In 1989, there were just 6 pages of boy-specific toys, with 10 pages of girl-specific and 21 pages for either.

## WHAT MAKES PARTICULAR TOYS COLLECTABLE?

In deciding which toys to collect, in the field of figures and models alone the collector is faced with an amazing variety. There are endless specialities: Citroen, for instance, made and sold toy replicas of their cars to encourage brand loyalty when their owners grew up.

Above: *Ping medieval scene. Ping figures are not really toys, having been created for the adult market in historical models, mainly recalling the medieval era. Definition of what is a toy and what is a model becomes blurred when considering these figures, since they are rather stylized and toylike, although painted in matt paints. When these models are available, which is seldom, they sell for between £20 ($33) and £60 ($99) each. Phillips London.*

Right: *An early 'Hess' toy Hessmobile produced in Nuremberg. These toys were noted for their patent flywheel drive mechanism, and the high quality of lithography. c.1908, 8½ins (22cms).*

Children enjoy collecting more than most, and this is recognized by every manufacturer, from cigarette card makers upwards. Every manufacturer of toys that could be collected did their best to promote this aspect, so that the modern collector of old toys is best served, in ease of collecting, by starting on a series originally designed as a collectable for children, such as toy soldiers or die-cast toys.

Failing this, a framework is needed, such as a logical series to collect, for example, a catalogue with numbered lines, a manufacturer, a history, a process, or a specific theme of miniatures of a real-life subject. An

Above: *Action soldiers skiing in winter kit.*

important issue in setting the framework is understanding how much time and money is likely to be needed to acquire the collection, both in searching and buying. Some advice about this is given on pages 84–92.

The framework of the collection could be in the form of a story—perhaps the collector's view of the development of a type of toy, or his or her choice of what is most attractive and interesting within a selected field. The most difficult, inevitably, is to collect all known items in a field. The attraction of attempting a complete collection has lured many a collector but this presupposes that the extent of the complete collection is known, and this is where the research comes in.

Die-cast cars are particularly collectable simply because they often had annual catalogues issued, and documentation is relatively easy. The intricacies here are more to do with minute changes to manufacturing specifications, such as new colour patterns or types of tyre, creating new versions and thus giving an excuse to collect five examples of a Lesney Matchbox London Bus No. 5 rather than just one—or as many as seven, if the different advertizements on the sides are taken into account.

The history of particular toys is often bound up with the phenomenon of the 'craze', where a particular toy 'takes off' in sales with such rapidity that there is no keeping up with demand, every child having to have the toy in question. Such fads defy all logical attempts to extrapolate sales figures, and have led many a manufacturer to overextend their capacity just in time to fall victim to a total lack of interest in the marketplace. Cabbage Patch Kid dolls are a recent example of this.

Some types of toy have been more durable in nature, but the history of die-casts affords many examples of the introduction of new features causing agonizing re-appraisals among the competing firms in the industry. The power of television as an advertizing medium has caused some crazes to be even more instant than ever before, the annual marble and conker or 'killer' seasons being interspersed with sudden interludes of Mutant Ninja Turtle Heroes . . .

However, some of the more attractive toys that failed commercially through being overtaken by some other craze, have since turned out to be among the most rare and sought-after items for toy collectors. Some, on the other hand, have received the thumbs down from both contemporaries and collectors. How to spot the winners? A good possibility is that today's most attractive toys will become tomorrow's most attractive collectables.

In choosing the special themes of collectable toys to

cover in this book, many others have had to be left out. In the United States, for instance, cast-iron toys, pressed-steel toys, horse-drawn toys and paper toys (the equivalent of cheap plastic before plastic came into use), are often collected. British construction toys from Meccano to Lincoln logs and Lego are not yet much collected, but are so loved that they may become one of the good collectables of the future.

In the meantime, because toy collecting has become so popular, many toy manufacturers are producing models and limited editions aimed purely at the collecting market itself. Where these have been produced

Below: *Mattel's world-famous Barbie Doll, dressed to kill. Barbie's wardrobe and accessories have been regularly updated over the years to reflect current tastes and fashions.*

Above: *Robbie the Robot, by Nomura Toys of Japan, c.1956. 12½ins (32.5cms).*

by firms whose former products are widely collected, they have been generally successful, and some now command premium prices.

The choice of items for a collection remains subjective. There is no necessity to stick to any theme. Many toy manufacturers followed commercial opportunities and supplied parts for other industrialists. Tootsietoy, for instance, provided the die-cast playing pieces used for Monopoly. The sentry boxes for toy soldiers were sometimes lovely tinplate toys in their own right. Was G.I. Joe a soldier or a doll? With such a wide variety, each collector must decide what are, for them, the most amusing and attractive toys.

# DOLLS

*The well-loved child's doll now provokes much*

*interest among serious toy collectors, with*

*escalating prices to match.*

The most important advice to bear in mind when forming a doll collection is to select with taste and to acquire a good eye. A collection of quality rather than quantity should be the collector's aim.

In such a vast field as this there is the freedom either to focus upon particular types of dolls or those of a certain material, or to acquire examples of most types. Bisque, cloth, composition, celluloid, vinyl and wood were utilized either on their own or in conjunction with each other to produce dolls; hence each material forms an extremely interesting field for study.

Certainly, collecting bisque dolls, because of the material's surprising durability, continues to remain the most popular. Early celluloid has also begun to reach relatively good prices at auction (mostly for examples pre-1925), but little has survived in a perfect state due to its fragility.

If the collector is particularly interested in acquiring dolls for investment, then good-quality bisque-head dolls, pre-dating 1930, by Kämmer and Reinhardt, Simon & Halbig, Kestner, GBR Heubach, Baer & Proschild, Kley & Hahn and Bruno Schmidt are highly sought-after. Certain moulds manufactured by these firms are particularly rare and would make very exciting acquisitions.

The 'character' dolls, so called because the moulds were originally sculpted from life, were manufactured in France by S.F.B.J. (Société de Fabrication des Bébés et Jouets) and are currently fetching good prices at auction, depending on the rarity of the mould. These, too, are very collectable. Obviously the quality from doll to doll, even within the same mould number,

varies, due to the firing and subsequent skill in decoration of each head. Any imperfections such as kiln dust (brownish specks to the head), firing lines (resembling cracks and often blackened), lumps, uneven surfaces, or 'ruddy' complexion will devalue the doll. The extent to which the value is reduced depends entirely upon the overall effect such imperfections have, although generally speaking at least a third may be taken from the original value.

Damage in the form of hairline cracks, chips (earring holes are particularly susceptible) or wig pull (surface bisque damaged by removal of the wig) devalues the doll considerably, depending again upon the extent, but almost certainly by at least two-thirds. A very small hair-line crack to the rim of the crown or a tiny chip to the earring hole has a lesser effect upon the value of the doll, and a rare example or extremely interesting mould would still be a worthwhile acquisition, although by no means worth a top price.

The type of body and its condition are also important factors to consider when appraising a doll. Currently popular are the composition ball-jointed 'toddler' type, which were often used by Kämmer & Reinhardt, and also the chunky, ball-jointed all-wood or wood-and-composition French child body, particularly those stamped or labelled by Jumeau or S.F.B.J. (they are of excellent quality). A seriously damaged body would detract from the appeal of the doll and consequently

*Right: 'Peter', one of the highly successful and currently sought-after dolls from the Character series produced by Kämmer & Reinhardt. The downcast expression and fine modelling create a very realistic effect, coupled with a good quality ball-jointed composition body dressed in a wool and cotton sailor suit. The doll's head was in fact made by the porcelain firm Simon & Halbig in Germany.*

# DOLLS

*Right: A more commonly found, but nonetheless collectable, Character baby, with weighted blue eyes and laughing mouth. Of particular value is the bent limb composition body, which is of excellent quality and realistic in form. This example is marked 'K * R, Simon & Halbig 116/A', and is 15ins (38cms) in height. It was valued at auction in 1990 in the region of £1,100 ($1,815) and would be an excellent acquisition.*

*Below: This is an example of a Character doll manufactured by Armand Marseille in Germany. The features are crisply modelled, with painted blue eyes and closed mouth — clearly the expression of a happy child. This is a rare mould and few are seen at auction, which is reflected in the sale price; it sold for £3,300 ($5,445) at Phillips of London in 1989. This doll has an overall height (including the body) of 18ins (46cms), and is marked 'AGM'.*

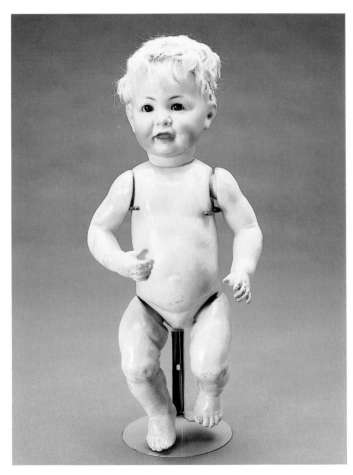

*Above: A very fine quality bisque head made by the firm of Simon & Halbig in Germany, modelled on more adult features with brown eyes, pierced ears and slightly parted, smiling mouth. The bisque is pale and smooth. The head alone sold for £500 ($825) at auction in 1990.*

its value, although a disjointed body, with all parts in good condition, would certainly be worthwhile acquiring as it may be restrung by an experienced restorer.

Great care in display is necessary for dolls of all materials. They should be stored in dust-free glass cabinets away from direct sunlight.

Cloth dolls form a very interesting collecting field and certainly good examples of the most renowned manufacturers would be essential in a representative collection. At the top end of the range are the highly desirable Art Dolls by Kathe Kruse (recently a Kruse child doll, 16 inches (40 cm) in height, fetched £1,000 (about $1,650) at Phillips in Scotland) and the all-felt character figures by Steiff of Germany, followed by Chad Valley, Norah Wellings and Deans Rag Book Co.

Composition and celluloid have a narrower range of interesting examples from which to choose and in investment terms neither area really matches up to the quantity and quality produced in bisque. Certainly the most interesting dolls are worthy of inclusion in a representative collection and prices for Kämmer and Reinhardt celluloid character moulds have risen steadily.

The term reproduction strikes fear in the heart of every collector, dealer and auctioneer. Of course, those which have been marketed truthfully as such can be of interest, although not to the purist. It is possible to purchase reproductions either in kit form

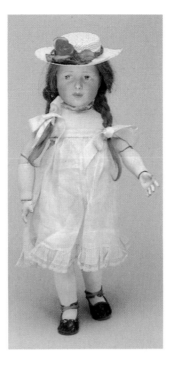

Left: *A rare Kämmer and Reinhardt bisque Character doll, German, c.1909, impressed 109 49, with closed smiling mouth, painted blue eyes looking to the right, red real hair plaits and ball-jointed wood and composition body in white dress and straw bonnet, 19¼ins (49cms).*

Above: *A Kämmer & Reinhardt bisque Character doll, German, c.1911, impressed 116/A 36, with curved limb composition body, open/closed mouth and simulated upper teeth, weighted blue eyes and red wig. 14ins (36cms) £1,760 ($2,765), Sotheby's London 1989.*

or already made up, and doll-making courses are available for those who wish to try the craft for themselves.

## IDENTIFYING DOLLS

The first step to take when appraising a bisque-head doll, whose manufacturer may not be immediately apparent, is to look at the rear of the head for any impressed or stamped markings. This will aid in determining the maker but not necessarily the age of the doll as particular moulds were continued for many years, often with no change. However, by careful study and thanks to the research undertaken into the many doll firms, it is possible to discover the date from which the maker patented certain moulds.

Generally, dolls of late manufacture tend to have a much redder complexion and the bisque has a coarser texture. Again, only by continual handling and inspection of dolls can assessments be made with any confidence. This knowledge can take years to attain, and the collector should always be prepared to seek a second opinion if unsure.

Sadly, sometimes fake dolls are sold to the unwary or less knowledgeable collector by unscrupulous or ill-informed individuals as 'antique' or originals. It must be remembered that no one is infallible and even those professing deep knowledge in this field have been caught out in their time. Extreme care when inspecting a possible purchase is necessary, and of course the collector who may be willing to spend several thousands of pounds or dollars on a particular doll would assess the example minutely. Thorough knowledge of doll markings (and the crispness of their impression) is of utmost importance, as is the size of the bisque head in relationship to the overall length: it is well known that moulds cast from an original shrink a percentage of the correct size. Poor artistry in decoration would also indicate the possibility of a fake. As artists were employed to paint one particular area of the head, be it lashes, brows or lips, etc., the proficiency was of very high standard and the brush strokes indicative of a confident, sensitive hand. Original bisque heads may be found with a new body, and although these are not fakes, caution must be exercised and the value is obviously reduced.

Many dolls were dressed by the firm which produced them, and obviously those retaining their original costume in good condition are highly sought-after (particularly those still within the original box). It is often difficult to assess whether the costume is original or just contemporary to the period of the doll. Reproduction costume is commonly found on dolls, and if antique fabrics have been used this can be difficult for the untrained eye to detect. The most useful advice to offer is for the collector to compare with examples already in existence, either by visiting museums, regular viewing of auction sales and studying the

Right: *The Simon & Halbig 'lady' doll on the far left of this photograph gives an indication of the type of body used for this particular mould, with adult female proportions. The colour of the eyes (blue) make it a slightly more desirable acquisition than brown-eyed models of a similar type. The head is still mounted on its original composition body, thus achieving a figure of £1,500 ($2,475) at auction in 1990. Its companions to the right are not Character dolls — the central example is a rare Jumeau phonograph (talking) doll. Manufactured from 1895, she has five cylinders by Lionet singing Spanish airs, consequently adding to the value; she sold, complete with original box, for £4,800 ($7,920) at auction in 1990. The doll to the right is a German bisque-head doll of unattributable manufacture; the head is of fairly good quality but has a slight 'rub' to the cheek, spoiling its effect — it was valued in 1990 in the region of £300 ($495).*

Above: *Three Kämmer & Reinhardt Character dolls, German c.1911, all impressed 115/A; 19ins (48cms), 13½ins (34cms) and 19ins (48cms). £2,970 ($4,665), £1,980 ($3,110) and £3,740 ($5,870), Sotheby's London 1989.*

catalogues produced, or by reference to the many publications on the subject.

Reproductions or fakes of dolls in categories other than bisque are found less frequently, although paper cut-out dolls with lithographed colour are greatly reproduced today. Close inspection of examples will reveal the modern printing process.

## RESTORING DOLLS

Whenever possible it is always advisable to leave the doll in as original a state as possible. The bulk of dolls which have survived have been restored somewhere along their history, most often re-wigged, re-strung or re-dressed. Certainly at auction, heavily restored dolls are offered at figures below those which could be expected for an unrestored example in good condition. It is a great shame that old dolls are often forced to appear in new pristine condition with a shining wig, contemporary fabric made up to a period design costume, replaced lashes, new eyes and re-painted body.

Restoration is an art on its own which should only be undertaken by a recommended professional. It is very costly, which can be off-putting, but if the doll in question is of sufficient rarity and value to warrant attention, and the restoration would enhance it both aesthetically and investment-wise, then the fee is worthwhile.

Possibly the worst form of restoration undertaken by the inexperienced is redecoration of the head. Any touching up of the doll reduces its value. Hairline cracks or chips may be carefully removed, but again, while the overall appeal of the doll will increase, its value will not, and such work is better left to the experienced restorer. There are numerous doll hospitals and dealers who undertake restoration, although it should be noted that occasions have arisen where a doll sent to be re-strung has returned with a redecorated head and overpainted body! Simple restoration than to replace the missing piece with one of new manufacture, or to replace the whole body. Overpainting a body is unnecessary unless the condition is extremely poor—a sensitive eye with an appreciation for age will always show a preference for an original if slightly worn body.

Upon acquiring an old doll, it may be necessary to gently clean the head, which can be done easily with careful application of cotton wool and a little ordinary hand soap. In fact, this procedure proves useful in distinguishing between bisque imperfections and dust.

When deciding to re-costume a doll, research is necessary into the type of outfit which the example would have worn, and the most useful source for reference, other than visiting museums, is to consult Coleman's *Collectors' Encyclopedia of Dolls' Clothes*. Great pleasure can be derived from costuming dolls, and, provided the correct design and antique fabric are used, the overall effect can be very good. Patterns are available to aid the dressmaker in construction which can be obtained through doll shops and magazines. Antique textiles can be purchased from dealers, who often have a box of end cuts and pieces of hand-made lace. Otherwise, the auction room is often a good place to look, and it is possible to buy complete period dolls' costumes from auctions too—often many garments are included to make up a lot and may include whitework, undergarments and linen, as the dolls were

Above: *Two Kämmer & Reinhardt bisque Character dolls, German, c.1909, the boy impressed 101 43, the girl impressed 109 39, both with composition and wood bodies. 17ins (43cms) and 15½ins (39cms) £2,310 ($3,625) and £4,620 ($7,255), Sotheby's London 1989.*

such as careful cleaning, re-wigging, re-stringing and dressing may be undertaken by the collector. Courses in re-stringing dolls are available, and attending one of these is much better than following diagrams found in publications. It is vital to use the correct elastic and not to string at too great a tension, as this could result in a cracked head.

When considering re-wigging an old doll, care must be taken in deciding whether the original was mohair, flax or real human hair. The correct type may be purchased from most dealers. By no means should acrylic versions be used, as these would ruin the effect of the doll. Most collectors probably have various stored wigs from which to choose.

Replacement bodies or parts of the correct type and age for the doll in question may be purchased from dealers or are sometimes included in a lot at auction. It is far better to search for the correct part

Above: *A fine rare J.D. Kestner glass-eyed bisque Kewpie doll, German, c.1913, impressed O'Neill, JDK 10. 10½ins (27cms) £3,520 ($6,230), Sotheby's London 1989.*

*Above: 'Moritz' is a well known fictional German character produced by many doll firms, including Kestner. It has moulded and painted hair, with intalgio, that is incised, blue eyes. The body, although not of very good quality, was effectively costumed at a later date. Despite the chip to the quiff and rear of the head, this doll fetched £1,800 ($2,970) at auction in 1990.*

*Above: This is a typical example of the type of work produced by S.F.B.J. in France during the first quarter of the 20th century. Note the upward-looking weighted eyes, a common feature of S.F.B.J. dolls; many examples exist which are quite speckled and grainy to the touch. The good wig and costume make this particular doll a worthy acquisition.*

costumed precisely as their young owner would have been. Prices are often high, as original costume is greatly sought-after if of good quality and condition. Obviously, restoration of costume is to be approached with great care and necessary cleaning should be gentle, avoiding use of harsh detergents at all costs.

Luckily there are many doll clubs which can assist the collector in gaining knowledge, advising on restoration procedures and putting him or her in contact with other collectors. Certainly reading as many books as possible on the subject helps the collector to learn about the history of manufacturers, types of dolls, and why certain dolls become popular as a result of social circumstances. Magazines are useful for obtaining names and addresses of dealers, restorers and forthcoming fairs, and contain many useful articles with new information for the collector, as well as highlighting current trends in the field. Doll fairs are also an ideal venue for the purchase of dolls from dealers and are excellent for the variety on offer.

Of course regular viewing of auction sales enables the collector to see the changes in the market and to understand why certain dolls achieve very high prices. Regular sales are held worldwide and catalogues (mostly illustrated), which contain printed estimates for each lot, are circulated beforehand. Prices at auction tend to be lower than those of retail; therefore it is possible to buy extremely interesting examples for a lower price than usual, although some restoration may be necessary. Certainly there is a wide variety of types and ages on offer, and buying at auction can be very exciting.

At the end of the day, however, the acquisition of a doll should be one of personal choice, irrespective of fashion and only governed by cost, quality and taste. The true collector does not buy with a view to possible future financial gain but for the pleasure derived both from learning about the subject and from the objects themselves.

*Right: Lenci dolls form a wide and very absorbing collecting field of their own, and examples in good condition, fully marked — either with 'Lenci' inscribed on the sole of the foot, or tagged — and dating from the early years of production, have fetched from £100 ($165) upwards at auction.*

# DOLL'S HOUSES

*Doll's houses are not only good investments;*

*since they are mostly constructed for childhood*

*pleasure and education, their appeal to the*

*collector is also due to our fascination with the*

*miniature, and to their historical, decorative*

*and representative value.*

Few doll's houses of outstanding quality have survived from the early years of the twentieth century. Therefore prices for examples in good condition are, not surprisingly, high. The collector is advised to choose with care and to search for quality. This may take longer than in some other collecting fields, but is ultimately extremely satisfying when 'the' house is discovered. From the outbreak of World War II until the last decade, doll's houses of fine craftsmanship were very rarely constructed, although there are one or two notable exceptions. There is no reason why the collector should not focus upon pieces made by contemporary craftsmen, of which there are outstanding examples.

This area of study offers a wide variety of subjects from which to choose and there are many themes on which the collector can concentrate. The most usual collections are organized around the type of material (wood, lithographed paper on wood, lithographed card and many more), or names of manufacturers (Leries, Tri- ang, Schoenhut, Hacker or McLoughlin among others). The collector may wish to focus upon German or French model rooms, which are a highly rewarding field for study, reflecting European social and educational characteristics, or may wish to represent virtually all manufacturers, thus tracing the history of doll's houses throughout the century. Doll's house furniture and miniatures also form an interest-

Above: *A printed paper-on-wood doll's house of three bays and two stories with a balcony to the first floor supported by four columns; the house opens at the front to reveal four rooms with staircase and landing, and original wall and floor papers, fireplaces and tin range. 26ins (66cms) wide by G.J. Lines c.1918. £300-£400 (c.$495-$660).*

Above left: *A large and elaborate doll's house, German, c.1900. The villa has brickwork of lithographed paper, and is well-detailed with architectural features, opening internal doors and original wallpapers and floor patterns.*

Above: *A painted wooden doll's house modelled as a Swiss chalet, of three stories, with red painted roof. Furnished, it is 21ins (53cms) wide, German c.1920, marked in pencil on the base 5604. £300-£500 ($495-$825).*

ing and easily displayed subject. Again, it is possible to purchase contemporary doll's house furniture and related items, made by excellent craftsmen, and there are frequent fairs devoted to these.

Doll's shops, especially those made of lithographed card, are extremely interesting, although relatively rare. Particularly collectable are those made in America by the firm of Bliss, and in Britain by Raphael Tuck.

As with any other collecting field, there are important factors to take into consideration when appraising a doll's house. Certainly, age, quality of construction, condition, manufacturer, standard of detail, decorativeness and cost are all to be considered. Ultimately the example will appeal because of its personal qualities; it is not a good idea to acquire a particular example just because it is old or manufactured by a well-known firm. Forming a collection is an individual choice and should not be subjective to fashion; certainly the most interesting collections are often those centred on a theme or reflecting the personality of the collector.

Condition is of great importance, especially when confronted by an example of a once-fine house, or one of famous manufacture. The item must be considered carefully as it may well be beyond restoration, and in fact may have little left of its original decorative appeal. Although it is preferable not to restore a doll's house to absolute perfection (often its original, played-with look can be part of the overall appeal to the collector), the aim should be to retain any outstanding characteristics and to enhance them.

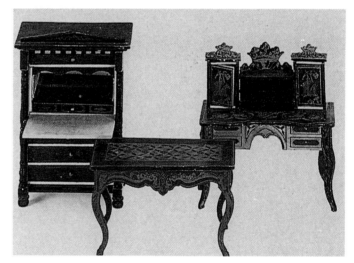

Above: *Three pieces of transfer-printed Waltershausen doll's house furniture, comprising plat du jour, lady's writing table and a bureau; and other doll's house items including a gong. £250-£300 ($413-$495).*

Although there are fine houses of unknown manufacture which would make excellent acquisition, there are certain firms whose work is particularly sought-after, due to their quality of construction, and their historical interest. The most collectable early doll's houses with decorative appeal are those by G. and J. Lines, Christian Hacker, R. Bliss and McLoughlin Bros. The original exterior and interior decoration must be retained in order for a high price to be paid. There are many examples with overpainted roofs or

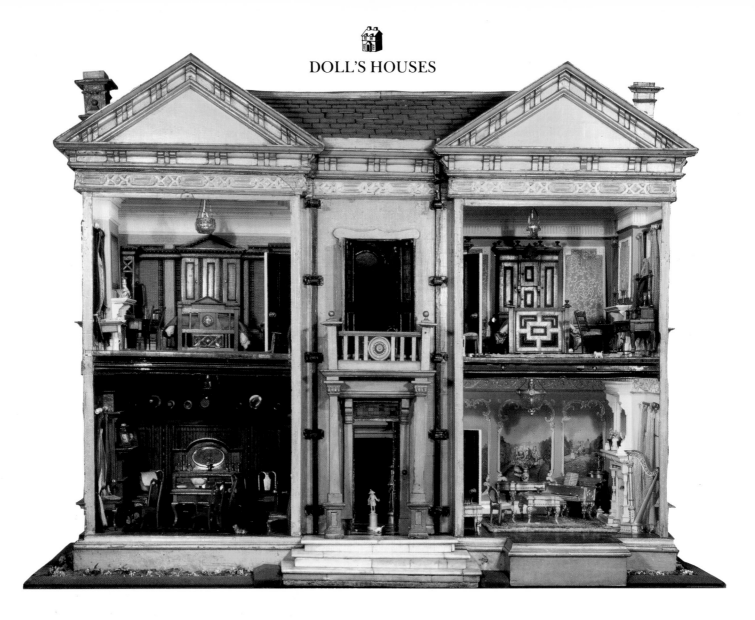

Top: *The Batty Doll's House. A unique and extremely fine construction, the house took 22 years to build. Pine was used for the superstructure of the house, and the well balanced exterior, of classical architectural lines, opened to reveal a superbly crafted interior.*

Above: *The Louis XIV-style salon perfectly illustrates the attention to every detail in the interior decoration of the Batty Doll's House, which includes a dining room, two bedrooms, a hall, landing and stairwell. The house sold for £6,800 ($11,220) at auction in 1984.*

repapered interiors, which would of course affect the value, as only those in virtually original condition are of very great monetary value (subject to design, age and manufacture).

Great care is needed in preserving a collection. Direct sunlight obviously causes colours to fade, and although a dry environment of stable temperature is required, central heating can cause a great deal of damage to doll's houses, warping the wood and causing cracks. Not surprisingly, doll's houses are susceptible to attack by insects, from moths to woodworm, and close inspection of a possible purchase is necessary to detect such parasites. A possible remedy which would alleviate these problems is to place camphor balls or (less pungent) cedarwood shavings inside the house.

It is obviously far easier to display room settings or model shops and miniature furnishings in glass dust-free cabinets, but the majority of doll's houses are too large for this. It is probably easier to set aside a separate room for the collection.

Alterations and restoration to a doll's house can result in devaluation of the example. If any restoration at all is necessary, it must be very carefully undertaken, with a view to enhancing the house rather than stripping it of any character.

An old doll's house may need careful cleaning when bought. A duster will remove any surface dirt, but a paintbrush or even toothbrush will be useful for nooks and crannies. At this stage, the extent of any woodworm damage may also be properly assessed. In fact, prior to purchase of a doll's house, the example must be thoroughly examined for signs of worm damage. If extensive, the price of the house must be considered carefully.

The interior is as important as the exterior, but to come across an example retaining its original furnishings is rare. Sadly, the various chattels are often sold separately by dealers and auctioneers, although the better specialists see the folly in this.

Cracks, dampness, missing panes or architectural ornament, worn paintwork or signs of repainting must be observed and noted. Carefully inspecting the bottom of the house may reveal a maker's mark. Assessing a doll's house is similar to appraising furniture, where the collector is advised to stand back and survey the overall properties of the example. The correct balance of width to height is important, as is comparing the size of rooms to the house as a whole structure. Remember to think in terms of balance; if furniture is to be purchased it has to be of the right scale.

If the exterior has been overpainted, it may be possible carefully to strip the unwanted layer away and reveal the original. Of course, this may be a task better left to a recommended professional, which although costly, can give the collector the assurance that the safest cleaning materials are being used. Even the advice of a good furniture restorer would aid in the repair of a wooden example. Particular care must be

*Above: A floral papered suite of lithographed furniture, manufactured at the turn of the century, and of very good quality. The condition is remarkable, and to find such a complete set is a rarity. A set such as this will never lose its value, and these were valued at c.£500 ($825).*

taken with lithographed paper examples as their glory is in the colour and decorative design, which can easily be ruined by scratching or spotting with liquid.

It is important to remember that only unwanted later additions must be removed, to restore the house to as near its original condition as possible. Adding replacement pieces may make parts of the house look noticeably new; therefore it is better to leave the example alone, particularly if its future value is to increase or even be maintained. When considering the interior of a doll's house, the original wallpapers, if any at all, should always be kept, even though they

*Left: A suite of ornate gilt and silvered pressed metal furniture such as this is a rare find, and of equal interest to collectors primarily concerned with miniatures as well as to those wishing to furnish a doll's house. The detailed filigree work forming the structure of each piece is reflected in the value; the group as a whole has been valued at over £1,000 ($1,650).*

may appear worn or shabby. Not surprisingly, original papers add value to a house, and modern replacements detract both aesthetically and financially. A new acquisition may have a repapered interior, underneath which original and charming wall coverings may exist. Therefore it is wise, very tentatively, to attempt to remove the newer paper (remember always to seek professional help if there is any possibility of ruining a potentially fine doll's house with amateurish handling). Should the doll's house have none of the original papers it is possible to buy reproductions of the old types through a reputable shop. Such magazines as *Doll's House World* contain very useful addresses for obtaining information on restorers and restoration, as well as dates of forthcoming fairs, conventions, auction room news, research and clubs. Combing the advertizement sections of design publications such as *The World of Interiors, Traditional Homes* and others is a useful source of names and addresses of firms which manufacture reproductions of the old embossed wallpapers that decorated so many houses in the early twentieth century, fragments of which could be a successful replacement wall covering for a doll's house if absolutely necessary.

One of the most fascinating aspects of the field is that research into and knowledge of architecture and interior design is automatically linked to the subject, not only as an aid to dating examples (for instance, the 'colonial style' doll's house was widely popular in the 1920s, and 'stockbroker-style' tudor houses were common by the 1930s, as well as Art Nouveau and subsequently 'minimalist' interiors, in their own periods), but also as an aid in restoration. Obviously, for shop settings, research into the appropriate fixtures and fittings is important but, especially if collecting items to furnish a grocery store, foodstuffs and the packaging design thereof must be of the same period in order to recreate the correct atmosphere. Floors and ceilings must not be overlooked either, although many later houses will probably be carpeted —features that do not conform to the period of the interior, or which are too modern in colour, design and material and therefore likely to be a replacement, should be disposed of. It may be possible to discover original simulated tile or parquet flooring beneath, which even if fairly worn should be left alone. Although it may be felt that carpeting really falls into the category of furniture and chattels, to be discussed shortly, it may as well be pointed out now that not until the end of the 1930s did stair carpeting cover the entire tread; prior to this date a strip ran down the middle, with uncovered wood to either side.

Doll's house window panes are very susceptible to both loss or damage, and obviously replacement of these would enhance the aesthetic quality of the house. Old glass, suitable for houses dating from the early years of the twentieth century, may be easily cut from an unwanted picture frame of a similar date.

Right: *A painted wooden doll's house, of five bays and four stories, with a canopy over the central front door, bay windows on the first floor, and French windows leading to a balcony at the side. It opens to reveal ten rooms with hall, staircase and landings, interior doors, bathroom fittings, four side windows and contemporary wall and floor papers. 50ins (127cms) wide, 69ins (175cms) high and 16ins (41cms) deep, the front has been removed and attached to the back for exhibition purposes. £3,000-£5,000 (c.$4,950-$8,250).*

Left: *A street scene of wooden stable, doll's house and milk cart, dating from c.1880 to 1905. The well detailed wooden stable has a hay loft above and stalls containing two horses and a cart; the doll's house is decorated with lithographed paper on wood and has good architectural detail. The tinplate milk cart is by Marklin, and is delicately hand painted, containing a number of nickle-plated churns harnessed to a well modelled carved wooden horse covered in real pony skin. Stable 18ins (46cms), doll's house 19ins (48cms), and cart and horse 16ins (41cms).*

Of course, considering the furnishing of a doll's house is of great importance. It may not be necessary to collect furniture, fixtures and fittings all from the same period as the house itself, unless an effect totally in the idiom of that time is to be recreated. Many charming examples exist where the furniture dates from different periods, although obviously a 1950s-style table would seem quite at odds in an interior primarily of Edwardian decoration. Selective taste and careful attention to the tiniest detail are required for a successful decor, linked to an eye for quality.

### DOLL'S HOUSE FURNITURE
Doll's house furniture can form an absorbing collecting field on its own, and certainly prices at auction can be high for a suite of furniture in good condition and early in date. There are numerous contemporary craftsmen producing quite exquisite miniatures, reproducing earlier styles, which, although costly, are of such quality that their purchase is worthwhile.

As with a reproduction of any shape or form, a doll's house of age would not benefit by being furnished with such examples, and it is far more aesthetically pleasing to spend time, possibly years, acquiring original good quality furniture to decorate a house of value.

An interior that is too composed can be offputting, though, and often the most interesting examples are those with an almost lived-in atmosphere, expressing homeliness and warmth. There is a fine line between

Above: *A wooden doll's house, of three bays and two stories, with galleried roofs, the central door flanked by bays and surmounted by a balconied French window, 37ins (94cms) high by G. and J. Lines c.1910. This house has been repainted and redecorated. £800-£1,000 (c.$1,320-$1,650).*

Above: *A box-type wooden doll's house, the facade with brick paper on the ground floor and original cream paintwork above, with remains of gilt lines. The house opens to reveal four rooms, with varnished white wood pelmets, teak window sills and original papers on the inside of the facade. 24ins (61cms) high by G & J Lines, c. 1910. £200-£300 (c.$330-$495).*

As with doll's houses, the collector must take care in dating examples of doll's house furniture, as the same styles were often produced over a number of years, and it is all too easy to pre-date pieces unwittingly. Again, careful study of museum exhibits, regular viewing of sales and fairs (which also helps to keep in touch with current fashions and market prices), reading old trade catalogues and the numerous books and magazines published, all assist the collector to gain a 'feel' for this subject and to sift the quality from the inferior, as well as to help with identification. Furniture was often stamped or incised, which makes attribution possible. Unmarked examples must be viewed with caution and carefully compared to already accounted-for examples.

Above: *The Calke Abbey Doll's House: a 19th-century doll's house in the style of a 17th-century building. Unlike many of the other subjects covered in this volume, the history and production of the doll's house precedes the 20th century, although, as they are so often reproductions of period homes, the style of the house should not be used as a firm indicator of the date of manufacture.*

a doll's house or room as a child's toy and those constructed and decorated for adult pleasure. It is very important to try to equip a doll's house with furnishings of the correct scale, as oversized or undersized items do not contribute well to the overall balance.

Doll's house furniture may be purchased from reputable dealers, at fairs or auction room sales. Prices can be very high for good quality, and names to look out for are Elgin, boxed sets of Tootsietoy furniture, Lines Bros Ltd, Marklin, Ulgo, stylish Art Nouveau and Art Deco pieces and Bliss. Foodstuffs, glassware, silver and other chattels are also highly sought-after if of good quality and condition.

# TINPLATE TOYS

*Tinplate toys enjoyed huge popularity*

*throughout Europe and America for well over*

*100 years until the 1960s, which saw the end*

*of quality tin toy production. Today those same*

*toys are eagerly sought-after by millions of*

*collectors and dealers worldwide.*

It is surprising to remember that as recently as the early 1970s there was precious little public interest in old tin toys, and the few collectors that did exist had little or no difficulty in obtaining them. Indeed, the only difficulty the collector faced then was halting the destruction or junking of the toys before he or she got to them, whereas today, merely twenty years later, it is the scarcity and cost of the toys that can present difficulties to the collector. Nowadays, collectors are often prepared to pay quite large sums of money to own a particular example that appeals to them. Specialist tinplate toy fairs and collectors' auctions are now commonplace, while toy collectors' clubs and societies publish a wide range of books and periodicals to satisfy the evergrowing demand for information on antique and tinplate toys.

Toys manufactured from tinplate are known to have been available in Europe since the 1830s, and examples were exhibited in Britain at the Great Exhibition of 1851. These would have been very expensive toys, hand-made by highly skilled tinsmiths and painted by outworkers, and were probably only purchased for extremely fortunate children or as executive toys for the amusement of the head of the family. By the turn of the twentieth century Germany and, in particular, Nuremberg, had emerged as the centre for much of the world's tinplate toy trade, being the home of such famous marques as Bing, Carrette and Ernst Plank. Another famous German maker, Marklin, had established its factory in Goppingen. The products from these factories were superbly well made from tinplate, usually with strong clockwork mechanisms, and finally decorated and lithographed with fine details and strong colours.

Above: *A Marklin tinplate Car Construction Set No.1108 G, comprising chassis and bodywork for a Pullman limousine and an armoured car. c.1935.*

The range of tinplate toys was extremely varied in both price and type, and included the popular 'penny toys' as well as the more expensive products. The Gamages of Holborn toyshop catalogue for 1911 included a comprehensive range of seventeen German-made tinplate vehicles with prices ranging from 4 old pence to 35 shillings, such as a 'Mechanical Motor Car, propelled by momentum of fly wheel, 4d' or 'Motor Car, finely poly-chrome japanned by hand, with strong clockwork, rubber tyres, plastic seats and sacking box, very fine, solid finish with driver's front axle, adjustable for straight and circular runs, 7½ in long, 2/4½d'. The catalogue included motor buses (with British advertizing including Pears soap and Oxo), taxi-cabs, fire engines, 'Clockwork Motor Car attacked by bull' and 'clown in Motor Car'. The top-of-the-range clockwork vehicle described must have been an absolute beauty: expensively priced for its day at 23/6d, 'the Motor Cab [was] finely japanned, elegantly finished, with very strong clockwork, driver with fur rug, pneumatic rubber tyres, steering, gear and brake, doors to open, one figure inside, four lanterns, and spare rubber types, 16¼ in long, 8 in wide, 9¾ in high'. What a toy! Probably manufactured by Carette, this tinplate toy would realize a few thousand pounds or dollars at auction today if it were in good condition.

Apart from motor vehicles, the range of tinplate toys also included aircraft, boats, trains, novelty subjects, animals and insects; each lithographed and decorated in colours, and tremendously enjoyable as playthings.

Above: *A post-World War II clockwork novelty toy motorcyclist and passenger produced in Japan by Kanto Toys of Tokyo. c.1950, 6ins (15cms).*

After World War I had taken its toll of Europe and her nations, the initiative to produce toys passed from Germany to Britain and America. By the 1930s Japan had also begun to produce reasonable tinplate toys, and Marklin, having survived the depression of the 1920s, emerged again as a great and innovative German toy producer.

Left: *Sentry boxes. Accessories for German solid-cast toy soldiers were often made of tinplate, and thus provide a bridge between the tinplate toy collector and the toy soldier collector. These beautiful examples of sentry boxes with British uniformed toy soldiers are meant to represent the Guards on foot at Buckingham Palace and on horseback at Whitehall, both in London. The scale of the foot soldier is twice that of the figure on horseback, and the foot sentry box is decorated in a continental pattern unlike that of London. Nevertheless they are superb examples of the German toymaker's art at a time when Britain was a major export market for toys from Germany. The foot guard with his box sold for £363 ($599), and the horse guard for £374 ($617) in 1987. Phillips London.*

Right: *Two Italian tinplate biscuit tins, modelled as a van and a coach. c.1960, 12ins (30cms).*

### THE TINPLATE TOY CAR

Tinplate toy enthusiasts can usually adopt a theme for their collections, either by choosing a particular maker or subject, or by concentrating on a certain period. For example road-going vehicles are very popular among collectors, especially since Dinky, Spot-On and Corgi toy die-cast models can be collected in parallel. Tinplate motor vehicles have been produced as toys for almost as long as motor transport has existed; in fact it would be easy to trace the development of the motor car through the toys that it inspired.

A particularly good twentieth-century tinplate toy motor car is the Hessmobile, produced in Nuremberg in about 1910 by John Leonard Hess. The Hess company was founded by Mathias Hess in the mid-1820s and was inherited by his son, John Leonard, on his death in 1886. The Hess products of the early twentieth century are admired for their high quality of lithographic decoration and detail. The Hessmobile series of motorcars was styled after the racing cars of the period, and featured composition drivers and a very effective fly-wheel mechanism for propulsion. This extremely clever 'motor' worked in the following way: first the steering wheel is pushed down, thus disengaging the driving-spindle from the top of the front wheels. The starting handle protruding from the radiator grille is cranked and sets a lead flywheel spinning within the bonnet/hood, causing the driving-spindles to rotate at great speed. With the steering wheel returned to its original position the driving-spindles engage the top of the front wheels, thus

causing them to drive the car. It is great fun to watch this toy trundle across a wooden floor and it is easy to imagine the enjoyment an Edwardian boy or girl got from playing with it. Such toys are now rare and much sought-after by collectors who will pay up to a couple of thousand pounds ($3–3,500) for the privilege of owning a good example today.

Probably the most famous and best-known tin toy ever made was the P2 Alfa Romeo produced in the 1920s by C.I.J. (Compagnie Industrielle du Jouet) of Paris. Originally costing 35/–, in 1929, these large-sized clockwork cars were classic toys from a golden age in Grand Prix motor racing, and available in the national colours of competing countries, including British racing green and Italian red. Measuring nearly 21 in (53 cm) the toy Alfas boasted a very comprehensive specification which included treaded or smooth tyres on steerable wheels, brake drums, an Alfa Romeo badge above a finely meshed radiator grill, and highly detailed bodywork with bonnet/hood louvres and leather bonnet/hood straps. It was hugely popular as a toy with schoolboys throughout Europe and remains so today with collectors who value it at around £1,000 ($1,650).

More affordable and just as collectable is the popular and plentiful series of Tri-ang 'Minic' tinplate clockwork road vehicles produced by Lines Brothers in South London from the mid-1930s into the 1950s. The range of over 100 small models was successfully produced to a scale that allowed the cars to be used in conjunction with the 0-gauge railway sets of the day, and provided an alternative to the die-cast Dinky toy models. The series lends itself very well to collecting as it was fully catalogued during production and is now covered by many publications and histories, making it an ideal subject for specialization as almost every type of British car, van, lorry and bus is represented. They are very pleasing models, strongly constructed and beautifully finished in a variety of colours, with some, including the Searchlight Lorry and Tourer Caravan Set, having electric lights for extra realism. Like the Dinky toys of the same period, the Minic commercial vehicles carried sham advertizing stickers, such as the four express parcel delivery vans of the regional railway companies bearing advertizements for 'Tri-ang Pedal Motors', 'Tri-ang Dolls' Houses' and 'Penguin' aircraft. Interest in Minic tinplate toys is bound to increase before too long, resulting in them becoming harder to find and more expensive to acquire in the marketplace.

During the 1920s and 1930s the Japanese tinplate toy industry began to develop by imitating German toys. However, after global hostilities had ceased in 1945, it soon matured into an innovative and dominant industry supplying the tin toy world with a new era of ingenious products. As a result of this new competition from the East, German toy factories started to decline, and the mid-1960s most production

*Right: A pre-war German clockwork tinplate Schuco Examico 4001 sports car based upon the BMW 328. This clever toy features four forward speeds, and one reverse, and a finger-operated clutch. c.1935, 5¾ins (14.4cms).*

Above: *A fine group, gathered for sale at Phillips in London, including some from Ubilda.*

Right: *The P2 Alfa Romeo produced in France by C.I.J. This model has treaded tyres and is painted in the Italian racing colours. c.1929, 20¾ins (53cms).*

had sadly ceased. One by one the famous marques disappeared, to be replaced in the toy shops by unfamiliar Oriental makers' names, such as Alps, Ashi, Bandai, Ickiko, Linemar, Nomura, Taiyo and Tomy.

The Japanese tinplate toy cars of this period were mainly designed for the US market, and as a consequence imitated the popular American automobiles of the day, giving Uncle Sam's children battery-powered Fords, Cadillacs and Buicks to play with. The ever-inventive German toymakers had developed the clockwork mechanism to the limit, but the move to battery-power enabled the Japanese to produce even cleverer toys. A good example of this is the Ford Skyliner Convertible Sports Car manufactured by Nomura in the 1960s. When the power is turned on, the tinplate car, decorated in cream and red with

# TINPLATE TOYS

chrome trim, meanders around in a haphazard manner. The driver constantly moves his head to look behind to watch the trunk-lid open while the hood folds back into the trunk. Then, after a short while, the trunk opens to allow the hood to reposition itself over the driver again. This is all done at a frantic pace, which makes the toy great fun and very amusing. A cheaper example probably aimed at the German market is the 1961 Mercedes Benz 220s, which featured electric headlamps, perspex windscreen, lithographed interior and chrome trim. Most of these Japanese battery-powered toys are fairly common and inexpensive. It is still usual to find them complete with their original sales boxes, and they will undoubtedly increase in value as their popularity increases among tinplate and toy collectors.

## TINPLATE TOY AIRCRAFT

Aircraft and ships have also been subjects of attention for the tinplate toymakers, and like the toy motor car examples, it is possible to trace the development of these forms of transport during the twentieth century. In the case of aircraft, or more accurately 'lighter-than-air' craft, the toys influenced by these flying machines were toy representations of the very latest inventions. As early as 1910, Marklin of Germany had produced a tinplate balloon inspired by Count Zeppelin's huge constructions. This was followed in 1915 by a clockwork toy Zeppelin (produced by Lehmann) which could be suspended from a length of string and was powered by an over-sized propeller assisting the toy realistically to achieve flight. Not surprisingly, this type of toy was very popular in its day and good examples today are both rare and expensive.

During the 1930s Frank Hornby's Meccano factory, together with Marklin, produced a series of kit-form tinplate constructor aeroplane sets. Meccano's literature for the outfits promises that 'You will never grow tired of building and running the superb models that you will be able to build. Your days will be full of fun and thrills!' The Meccano sets enjoyed a limited success, and while not being as realistic as the Marklin examples, they do capture the spirit of aviation at that time. The No. 1 constructor aeroplane, which originally cost 3/3d, resembled the Gloster Gauntlet fighter bi-plane and was available with a clockwork motor. The No. 2 constructor aeroplane was a larger set which allowed various types of aircraft to be produced by using a selection of interchangeable parts. The aircraft were either finished in camouflage or blue and cream with British national markings, except the sets for export which incorporated corrugated body and wing sections. These constructor aeroplane sets are collected by both Meccano and toy aircraft enthusiasts and represent modest value. Inevitably, the Japanese manufacturers also produced tinplate toy aircraft, doing so in their usual innovative way and using battery power.

Below: *Produced in Germany by Georg Kellermann & Co of Nuremberg, this tinplate clockwork aeroplane rolls from side-to-side as it travels along the floor and 'fires' sparks from its machine-gun. c.1930, 7¼ins (19cms).*

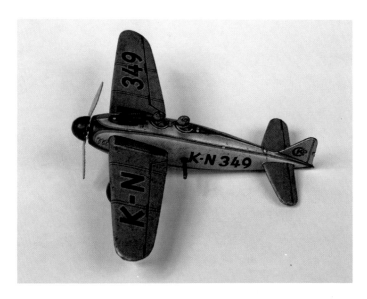

## TINPLATE BOATS

Tinplate toy boats, because of their very nature, are both rare and highly valued. They are among the most beautiful and desirable of all toys. Usually they had to be waterproof and were often difficult and very expensive to produce, requiring watertight soldered joints and thorough painting. Inevitably, many of these toys either sank, rusted, got broken or were

TINPLATE TOYS

Above: *Four Japanese tinplate battery-powered aircraft including a Bristol Bulldog by Straco, an Astro-Copter by Tomiyama, a Pan Am Boeing jet airliner by Linemar Co, and a United Airways DC7 four-engined mainliner with remote 'U-control'. All c.1958.*

Left: *A large, early 1920s clockwork tinplate ocean liner by Bing of Nuremberg, Germany. 25ins (64cms).*

Right: *Produced in Horsforth, Leeds, by Sutcliffe Pressings Ltd, the Unda-Wunda diving submarine was designed in the 1930s. It was a very popular toy which later became 'Nautilus', the submarine from Walt Disney's '20,000 Leagues Under the Sea'. 9½ins (23cms).*

Below: *'Kronprinzessin Cecillie', a rare painted tinplate display model of the Norddeutscher Lloyd line ocean liner, by Fleischmann of Nuremberg, c.1907, 60½ins (154cms) long. This is thought to be the largest toy ship ever built and was valued by Christie's South Kensington in 1989 at between £12,000 and £18,000 (c. $20,000 to $30,000).*

TINPLATE TOYS

simply thrown away, making toy boats the rarest of all toys collected today. Even the examples that have survived will probably have been restored or have replacement parts, because original fittings such as lifeboats, anchors, masts and flags were fragile and vulnerable to damage.

The best tinplate toy boats were produced in Germany between 1900 and 1920, usually using clockwork or steam mechanisms for power. Bing and Marklin, together with Fleischmann and Carette, produced a range of toy boats of all shapes and sizes that included liners, merchant vessels, naval craft and submarines. Some of these toys, such as Marklin's model of the *Mauretania* (sister ship to the *Carmenia* and the ill-fated *Lusitania*, which was torpedoed by the German Navy in 1915), were truly impressive and can be worth several thousands of pounds or dollars today. Produced in Goppingen around 1910, the detailed model measured over 38 in (95 cm) in length and would have cost the equivalent of about one month's pay for the average worker.

At the same time, Hess made some interesting clockwork toy battleships, designed for the mass market. They have three eccentric wheels concealed beneath the hull, giving a fairly realistic and amusing pitching-and-rolling effect.

During the 1930s a wide range of simple robust tinplate toy boats were made in England. These are still plentiful and affordable, making them a good area around which to form an interesting collection. Meccano of Liverpool and Sutcliffe Pressings of Leeds produced a number of toys that were inexpensive and popular for many years. The Hornby range of speedboats, such as the 'Hawk' and 'Racer III', were driven by good clockwork motors that could run for over five minutes.

The Sutcliffe factory closed in 1982, after producing fairly simple, but excellently produced, tinplate toy boats since the 1920s. Early examples of the firm's products had begun to be collectable while the company was still trading. In acknowledgement of that fact, Sutcliffe reproduced their 'Valiant' battleship in a limited edition to commemorate the bicentenary of their first boat which appeared in 1928. The interesting diversification into the commemorative market was followed up in 1981 when the company issued a small cruiser called 'Diana', named after the Princess of Wales, complete with a special box.

In the 1930s Bassett-Lowke of Northampton complemented the products of Meccano and Sutcliffe by producing some fine scale-model boats that are equal to the German examples. These were sometimes quite unusual models, including tugs, oil tankers and steam launches, well detailed with hand-rails, lifeboats, masts and ventilators, and powered by either clockwork or electric motors.

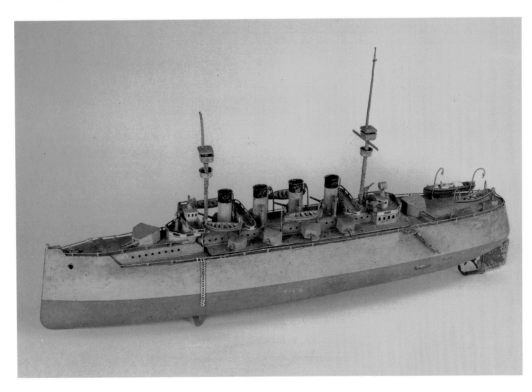

Above: *German, c.1912. A Bing four-funnelled battleship with clockwork mechanism.*

39

Above: *Robot toys have appeared relatively recently on the collecting scene, but already fine examples manufactured 40 years ago and less are fetching high five-figure sums at auction.*

Above: *The robot toy Nando, produced by Opset in Italy, c.1948. This example was sold by Christie's Amsterdam for D.fl. 4,255 (£1,216/$2,006) in May 1988.*

## OTHER TINPLATE TOYS

Tinplate toymakers of the twentieth century did not, of course, only use transport for inspiration for their toys. They took ideas from animals, sport, nature, people, and their own imaginations to invent and develop commercially successful toys. Animals, birds and fish were particular favourites of the German makers, and appeal to children and adults worldwide. Toy animals were personified to carry out human activities, like the tinplate clockwork car produced in the 1920s by Johann Distler of Nuremberg, with its monkey driver who raises and lowers his hat as the car is driven forward. The Japanese copied and continued the animal theme, using battery power, producing toys such as the 'Duck One-Man-Band' by Alps Shoji Ltd of Tokyo, in the late 1940s. The duck's eyes light up as it plays two side drums and cymbals above a bass drum. Toys like these are still modestly priced and collected by enthusiasts of novelty products.

Model people were also widely represented by tinplate toymakers around the world, especially specific persons with specific jobs. In 1910 Lehmann of Brandenburg, Germany, produced the very clever and hugely popular 'Gustav the Busy Miller' toy. Working on the simple principle of opposing volumes and gravity, Gustav climbs to the top of his windmill and then comes back down again with a sack of flour upon his head, so causing the sails to rotate. Equally popular in its day, though still modestly priced today, is the rather crude and colourful 1935 'Doughboy tank' by the New York maker, Louis Marx. Loosely based upon the British Mark II tank of World War I, a hatch at the rear opens to reveal a marksman who aims his rifle upwards and then returns inside the hatch. The toy tank, which is of tab and slot construction, is a good example of Marx toys. Marx became the largest toy manufacturer in the world.

Today, it is still possible to purchase new tinplate toys in British toy shops, although they are little more than inferior copies of German and Japanese tinplate toys, produced in Russia, Czechoslovakia, Hungary and China. These are certainly worth purchasing if a certain tin toy example is either too expensive or rare to obtain as an original. In the more developed countries after the 1960s most toys were produced out of plastic, which is probably a better material for modern living requirements. Naturally there are already collectors of early plastic toys!

## ROBOTS

The most recent field of tinplate toy collecting is that

Below: *A Jupiter robot by Yonezana, valued at between $4,000 and $6,000 (£2,424 and £3,636) by Christie's New York in November 1989.*

of robots. Robots, or mechanical men, have exerted a fascination on children and adults alike since the term was invented by the Czech Karel Capek in 1921. It derives from the Czech word 'Robota' for statute labour, and originally described organic artificial men. However, the word soon entered the science fiction and now engineering vocabulary as a description of a human-mimicking mechanical contrivance.

Toy robots derive mostly from science fictional models, but their forebears are toy automata. The interest in space travel and science-fiction since the early 1950s has led to robots and space toys. The early examples were probably based on Robbie the Robot from the 1956 film *The Forbidden Planet*. However, as the design developed, the robots became more personal creations based on science fantasy. Using battery power, the robots developed flashing eyes, individual movements, speech, and noisy flashing guns or lasers. Some have tin heads that open up to reveal grotesque rubber aliens' heads with illuminated eyes and nostrils. Others have bodies with hatches that open up for crackling, flashing guns to emerge from within. Enthusiasts will purchase modern examples straight from the shelves of toy shops, thus ensuring perfect examples complete with instructions and sales packaging.

Above: *A giant robot, 16ins (41cms) high, believed to be by Horikawa. It is battery operated, has moveable legs, and its chest opens to reveal a flashing gun.*

# TEDDY BEARS

*The battered teddy bear of childhood can now*

*be a highly sought-after and valuable*

*acquisition.*

Since the beginning of the last decade prices for teddy bears pre-1940 in date have spiralled upwards. Towards the end of the 1980s astonishing figures of up to £50,000 ($82,500) were seen in the auction rooms. Also during this period teddy bears of a very mixed state were fetching somewhat inflated prices just because they were old examples. The collector of teddy bears (the arctophile) must become interested in quality and not feel that every dearly loved bear is a worthwhile acquisition.

A teddy bear of outstanding quality and condition pre-dating 1920 and of unusual colour is worth buying, certain manufacturers being highly sought-after. The names to look out for are Steiff, Bing, Herman, Schuco (German); Ideal, Columbia (American); Chad Valley, Farnell, Merrythought and Deans (English). Prices for teddy bears have now begun to level out, thankfully—illustrating that collectors are choosing only examples of the best quality.

Teddy bears which are fully attributable to one of the more famous firms, particularly Steiff, are obviously of great interest to the collector. However, bears in poor condition, even by this firm, are not a desirable acquisition.

At the top end of the range are the early examples by Steiff, with their swivel-jointing at the neck, shoulder and hip, floss-stitched claws, felt-covered pads, hump back and excelsier filling.

Good-quality teddy bears can be purchased from reputable specialized dealers and the major auction firms. It is possible to find very worthy examples at local jumble sales, general auction rooms and markets, but the current upsurge in prices in this field has meant that it is difficult to acquire good examples for a small price as the general public has now become more aware of the possible value of teddy bears. Collecting modern bears is easily done by visiting major stores with good-quality toy departments. Limited-edition Steiff bears or examples with unusual innovations are available from such shops and are interesting acquisitions. They will no doubt be the collectables of the future.

There are major world-wide teddy bear conventions, which are an excellent source not only for the purchase of bears but also for keeping in touch with retail prices (somewhat higher in general than those at auction). Listings of future events and teddy bear clubs can be obtained through magazines devoted to this collecting field. Such publications contain lists of teddy bear dealers and auction rooms selling bears, as well as informative articles relating to current events in this field or new research and addresses of teddy bear hospitals and restorers.

Right: *This rare Steiff black mohair plush teddy bear was one of only 494 ever produced; they were a special order for the English market, manufactured in about 1912, in sizes ranging from 14 to 19ins (36 to 48cms). The black button eyes are mounted on red felt discs. Obviously condition is important, and this example has motheaten, though original, felt pads and some areas of sparse fur. An example at a Phillips auction in autumn 1990 was valued at £6,000-£10,000 ($9,900-$16,500).*

Above: *A charming group of teddy bears. On the left is a white-plush Steiff bear, c.1920; the tiny 3½in (9cm) bear — a very unusual size — is also by Steiff, c.1950, as is the bear in the centre. The bear to the right is probably by Hermann, c.1920.*

Early Steiff bears, *c.*1903–1925, were designed with long limbs and long felt-covered pads so that when the bear is standing upright the forelegs reach virtually to midway down the hind legs. They were the first bears with central seams and sealing wax noses.

The condition of a collectable bear should be excellent, as the value in all teddy bears lies in its fur covering, which should be mohair and plentiful. Examples are devalued considerably depending on the extent to which the covering has become worn. The original pads (mostly felt on better-quality bears) must be intact and show no signs of moth damage, to which they are highly susceptible, and the floss-stitching used to define the snout and claws must be intact.

When appraising a teddy bear there are certain characteristics to look out for. Colours other than the common beige or gold of most bears are highly desirable. Later Steiff examples were made in white, black, dual tone, red, apricot and cinnamon. Early teddy bears either had boot button eyes or eyes of glass (normally black and amber). They also had small, wide-apart, rounded ears, and a pronounced floss-stitched snout (not necessarily in black).

## IDENTIFYING TEDDY BEARS

Many teddy bears were produced copying the Steiff characteristics—they were not intended as fakes, but the copying of a superior style was obviously their selling point. The collector must therefore exercise extreme caution when attributing examples to the firm, particularly where there is no ear button, which was the maker's trademark. Of course it has been known for Steiff tags to be applied to bears not of

Left: *A silver-plush Steiff teddy bear, c.1904, with metal button and factory tag to the ear, pink silk, stitched snout, and black button eyes, wearing a contemporary but unoriginal German sailor suit. 30ins (76cms).*

Above: *A very rare short-red-plush teddy bear with button eyes, once owned by Xenia Georgievna, Princess of Russia, in the early 20th century. Steiff, Germany, 1906-1909, 13ins (33cms).*

Above: *This teddy bear, c. 1909, has a large head with glass eyes, pointed snout and excelsier filling. The ears are noticeably triangular, and the torso and legs are longer than usual. The areas of sparse fur and re-covered pads are reflected in its fairly low auction value of about £200 ($330) in 1990.*

Above: *A light-brown-plush teddy bear with boot button eyes and elongated limbs, 21ins (53cms). Steiff, c.1905, estimated by Christie's in 1989 at between £300 and £400 (c.$500 and $660).*

their manufacture and sold as such. It is up to the collector to do his or her homework and, if in any doubt, seek a second opinion. Steiff examples, as already noted, can be identified by the button in the left ear, and can also be dated this way, as the lettering design, as well as the metal colour and size, changed over the years. The earliest button bore the elephant trademark in *c.*1905 and was shortly followed by buttons inscribed 'Steiff' in capitals, with the last 'f' forming a continuous line beneath the preceding letters. Italicized script was introduced last. The pewter-type buttons pre-date the chrome examples, which were then followed by a brass type (grey buttons date from the late 1930s). The labels attached alongside the button infrequently survived on the earliest examples. Their colours, where they have survived, help to date them: white pre-dates 1926, red 1926–34, yellow 1934 onwards; white and yellow, or black and white, being found on those of contemporary manufacture.

A great deal of useful information was contained in the number code found on a Steiff label, which denotes the style and type of bear to which it is attached. The most informative research to date on the firm has been published as a book, *Button in Ear*, by Vurgen and Marianne Cieslik. This volume is highly recommended, containing pictorial examples of the Steiff products and advice on how to decode the numbered

Above: *Aloysius, an orange-plush teddy bear, probably German, c.1907, who received his name when he won the starring role of Sebastian Flyte's companion in the TV version of Waugh's Brideshead Revisited.*

Above: *A pale-golden mohair-plush-covered teddy bear to the left, probably English, 21ins (53cms), and a golden-plush-covered bear with elongated arms, 21ins (53cms).*

labels, as well as an historical account of the firm.

The best way to learn about teddy bears is not only through background reading but also by continual handling, especially of good quality Steiff, Bing and Hermann bears. As even the Steiff firm would use up old stock tags on occasion, it is possible unwittingly to date an example earlier than its actual manufacture. The points here, therefore, can only serve as a guide, as it is extremely difficult to make precise rules for dating Steiff teddy bears.

The firm of Glor Bing, in Nuremberg, are renowned for their mechanical bears, which are highly sought-after by collectors and appear only infrequently at auction; particularly rare are examples in their original costume. Examples can be identified by a metal ear tag, marked G.B.N. until 1919 and B.W. after this date. The mechanical key-wound examples are inscribed also on the key-hole, which does not become detached like the ear tag. It is difficult to attribute an unmarked example. However, there are general characteristics: a small triangular head, a flatter nose than, say, Steiff examples, boot button eyes and mechanical articulation.

Teddy bears produced by Hermann are difficult to identify and are often mistaken for Steiff examples. Attribution must be undertaken with great care, but manufacture was begun *c.*1907, so a teddy bear purported to be from this firm must not be dated before then. Hermann bears are still being produced today and, along with contemporary Steiff examples, are a worthy acquisition, being of excellent quality and representative of current work.

## RESTORING TEDDY BEARS

There are many examples of teddy bears which have undergone restoration. The most commonly seen are amateur attempts with a home-made appearance; some of these may be successful but others horrify the purist. As teddy bears were manufactured with the intention of being toys, those having some signs of childhood play can be more appealing to the eye of a collector than a perfect example. However, it is possible to clean carefully a very dirty acquisition using the mildest of detergents, without drenching the bear. When brushing the fur, caution must be exercised, as the covering may be so delicate as to come away from the backing. Always be prepared to seek advice from experienced restorers, preferably a recommended individual; teddy bear hospitals also exist (names and addresses can be found in the many magazines devoted to the subject). Professional restoration, of course, can be costly, depending upon the extent to which the teddy bear is in disrepair. Eyes, both boot button and the glass type, are easily obtainable, although research needs to be undertaken in order to ascertain which type the bear would have had originally. It is difficult for the amateur to replace pads successfully, and at all costs the correct fabric should be used (in the case of Steiff bears, light-coloured felt was used). If the repair is to be undertaken personally, it is advisable not to remove the damaged pad but simply to re-cover the area with the correct material, be it felt, velvet or rexine. Restoring torn areas of the covering or actual holes poses a problem for the inexperienced. Patching the damaged area must be avoided; it does noth-

ing to enhance either the aesthetic appeal or overall value of the bear. Such areas are better left alone, and, depending upon their extent, may not spoil the appearance too badly. Torn areas can be fairly easily stitched up using strong thread. Of course, if the teddy bear in question is very valuable, professional restoration using the correct thread and technique is necessary.

Early teddy bears sometimes suffer from shifting of the excelsier filling and appear to be sagging somewhat. It may not be necessary to attend to this as it can contribute to the character of the example. Not all teddies were filled with excelsier, however, and it must be ascertained whether this straw-like substance (literally wood shavings), kapok, or a mixture of the two was used. Gently squeezing areas of the body ought to answer this—excelsier will feel quite hard and can be heard, whereas kapok is soft and silent. Later teddy bears were filled with other substances too (although excelsier and kapok continued to be used). To obtain the correct filling for the bear is fairly difficult, so the services of a teddy bear hospital or recommended restorer would be advisable.

The covering of teddy bears makes them susceptible to pest infection. Upon acquiring a new example the collector should examine the item carefully before deciding to display the bear alongside those already there. There are various methods for ridding teddy bears of insects, two good ideas being to freeze the bear in a sealed plastic bag for at least two days, or to use a moth-proofing spray.

Probably the best method for display of acquisitions, as with most antiques of a manageable size, is to place them within a dust-free glass cabinet, away from direct sunlight which could so easily fade the fur colour.

There are many books on this subject available for the collector. Of course, such reading makes more sense when examples are regularly handled and the collector actually begins to understand teddy bears and define good quality from that of indifferent standard. Regular viewing of the sales in major auction rooms is also a recommended way of acquiring knowledge, and museums devoted to childhood have a selection of teddy bears and are always worth visiting.

Below: *This rather charming group of teddy bears perfectly illustrates how each bear has its own unique 'character' and that no two examples are exactly the same. They are of varying ages, but pre-date 1920 and are from the Steiff firm. Several types of mohair texture may be discerned — the top right-hand teddy having curly hair, while the example immediately below has a more ordinary covering, and the companion to his right has noticeably longer mohair.*

# TOY TRAINS

*Toy trains are one of the most popular and commercially successful forms of plaything ever imagined. Famous and evocative names such as Hornby and Marklin continue to work their magic for collectors both of original models and modern reproductions.*

Birthdays and Christmases all over the world for over five generations have witnessed many youngsters (and some grown-ups) excitedly unwrapping and opening their ultimate toy—a train set. Even the most cursory glance around any toy shop, that haven of escapism and enjoyment, will show that today toy trains are just as popular as ever. Hornby and Marklin, for instance, still make a wide selection of modern and vintage model trains and railways, faithfully reproducing tank and diesel engines, steam locomotives and electric trains.

Toy trains became available from the 1840s and soon were an essential addition to any boy's playroom. The early examples would have been simple wooden pull-along carpet toys of Bavarian or American origin, with gaily painted carriages and vans, sometimes with a length of wooden track to run along. Often these crude toy trains appear so unlike the actual steam trains of the mid-nineteenth century that it becomes clear the maker had probably never seen a train in his life. By the 1870s the wooden toy train had been replaced by German- or French-made tinplate, and English semi-scale cast-iron types, comprising of a locomotive and tender, first and second carriages, or a tank engine with goods wagons and guard's van. While still being very simple, the tinplate toy trains were better proportioned, more realistic and attractive than their wooden ancestors. Toward the end of the century clockwork mechanisms and steam propulsion

were available, and at the 1900 Paris Exhibition the electric model railway was first properly introduced to the public.

### 1900–1914

The typical range of toy train products on the market at the turn of the twentieth century can be surveyed in the 1905 toy catalogue of the world-famous Gamages toy shop of Holborn in London. Within the trains, trams and traction engines section six various toy trains are available, including 'Massive American Type Express Locomotive with good clockwork', Price 10/6 postage 6d; 'Special Value. Pull Train', Price 4d, postage 1.5d; 'Carpet Locomotive, with very strong clockwork, in fine polychrome japanning, 5½ inches long, 3½ inches high', Price 6/1, postage 2d; 'Really good model Clockwork Locomotive. Enamelled in various colours', Price 10½d, postage 3d, and 'Train on rails, with regulated clockwork Train consisting of Locomotive, tender and one passenger car, circle and set of rails, 10-inch diameter, length of train 8½ inches, finely japanned. Price 4/5d, postage 3d.' These trains, especially the clockwork, would have been of German

*Right: A 2½-inch gauge 2-2-0 spirit-fired live-steam brass and tinplate locomotive by Ernst Plank of Nuremberg, Germany. c.1900, 7ins (18cms).*

# TOY TRAINS

Left: *Back: A Swiss tinplate gauge '0' electric 2-4-2 locomotive with twin overhead conductors, and two goods wagons, by Buco. c.1935. Front: A Bing gauge '0' tinplate clockwork G.W.R. passenger train set. c.1926.*

Below left: *A Marklin electric 0-4-0 locomotive, with second and third class passenger carriages, a goods van, and a guard's van. c.1930.*

Below: *An attractive tinplate railway station, probably by Marklin, c.1920. 23ins (58.5cms).*

society who had the money and space necessary to indulge in toy railways. The trains became more expensive to buy new as they developed into 'models' rather than toys, and dangerous enough to concern parents about their children playing with them un-supervized, especially with the sometimes unpredict-able live steam models. Perhaps it was these factors that led to the notion of the train as father's toy!

By 1900 five different gauges existed, from No. 0–1¼-inch gauge to No. 4–2¹³⁄₁₆-inch gauge (commonly known as 3-inch gauge). This standard set of gauges was introduced by Marklin at the Liepzig Spring Fair in 1891 and soon the other toy train manufacturers of Nuremberg followed suit. The Marklin Toy Company was founded by Theodor and Caroline Marklin in Goppingen in 1859, and today the company main-tains its record for being the oldest manufacturer of toy trains in the world. Tinplate toys and trains were produced in the 1890s and by 1914 the number of employees at the factory reached 600. Fritz Eugen Marklin, Theodor Marklin's grandson, was the last Marklin within the management company when he died in 1961. It is claimed by aficionados of Marklin that the history of the railways and the concept of scale can be traced in that company's products.

Gauge 1 and gauge 0 are the two most common scales that the collector is likely to come upon from this period. Gauge 1 is roughly the same scale as the standard size 2⅛-inch Britains' lead figure, while gauge 0 was introduced as a space-saving scale that enabled more compact and complex layouts to be de-signed around it. The locomotives came in three basic designs, the simplest having four wheels or 0-4-0 chassis, and the more upmarket eight-wheel 4-4-0 bogie chassis, or the ten-wheel 4-4-2 bogie chassis configurations. These came with four- or six-wheel tenders containing some form of imitation or moulded coal supply.

The locomotives were of conventional design with traditional steam engine features, including many fine or working details. A close inspection of a typical German tinplate clockwork toy locomotive reveals a cylindrical boiler and funnel, with dome and whistle. Behind the boiler is the cabin in which the two-speed and reverse mechanism rods are located. This facili-tated braking and reversing control from the track. The boiler and cabin sit upon the chassis with body-work arches or fairings over the driving wheels. The live steam models had a firebox hung beneath the cabin, and copper boilers complete with safety valves and working whistles. These models are usually easy to identify as the paintwork on and adjacent to the boiler will have deteriorated due to the tremendous heat produced while being used. It is very rare to find a model that has never been steamed; collectors would prize an un-steamed example very highly, although they may also suspect that some degree of restoration had been made to it.

manufacture, and up until World War I they dominated the market, overtaking even American production.

Nuremberg was the home of the German toymakers and here they manufactured products with nostalgic appeal that now are among the most collectable toys. The toy and model trains produced prior to the Great War by such famous makers as Bing, Carette, Karl Bub and Marklin today command high values among collectors.

The variety of toy trains available to the Edwardian boy would have been enormous. However, they were affordable only by the more wealthy elements of

Right: *An inexpensive gauge '0' German tinplate clockwork passenger train set including a simple station building. c.1930.*

The clockwork trains housed the key-wind mechanism in the chassis between the driving wheels, with the key-hole usually located in the wheel arches or chassis skirt on the right-hand side. The mechanisms were particularly strong and able to power locomotive, tender and two carriages with ease. Fortunately, they are also of simple construction and so are easy to repair for continued use today. The locomotives were decorated in enamels or paint, and the more upmarket products would have been appointed with boiler hand-rails, headlamps, lubricators and other brass fittings. Although the trains were manufactured in Germany, they were often finished in the liveries of the countries in which they were sold. The liveries produced for Britain, for example, will be of British regions with regional letterings on the matching tenders. The four most prominent British railway companies found represented are the G.W.R. (Great Western Railway), L.N.W.R. (London and North Western Railway), M.R. (Midland Railway) and L.S.W.R. (London and South Western Railway), although there were fifteen different British railway companies to choose from at the time.

A whole range of passenger carriages, goods wagons and vans were produced to complement the locomotives, together with railway accessories including tinplate stations and platforms made to scale. A particular favourite manufactured by Bing was 'Victoria Station' listed in Gamages' 1906 catalogue and priced at 9d. This was a small model, designed to be illuminated from within by candles and colourfully lithographed on both sides with architectural details and contemporary advertisements, including the ubiquitous 'Smith and Sons Bookstall'. Alongside their excellent trains and track accessories, Bing produced probably the most popular rolling stock of the period. Their tinplate passenger coaches with printed and painted decoration had opening doors on either side and a detachable roof, revealing a fitted interior with seats and compartment details; while a humble four-wheeled brake/goods van featured hand-painted decoration, centre sliding doors and a typically Germanic guard's look-out cabin complete with rear access ladder. Such attention to detail and articulation made these products firm favourites with yesterday's child as well as today's collector.

The firm of Gebruder Bing was founded in 1863 by Ignaz and Adolf Bing, and by the 1880s they were manufacturing tinplate toys and trains. The company expanded rapidly and by 1914 it employed over 5,000 people. Bing resumed production after World War I. However, the world slump of the 1920s proved disastrous and in 1932 a receiver for the company was appointed. Sadly, within the next two years, tinplate toy and train production at the famous factory ceased altogether.

There are some notable exceptions to the German domination of the toy train market in the period up to 1914, and these include the companies of Bassett-Lowke Limited, Ives Railway Lines and Lionel.

The Bassett-Lowke Limited company was founded in Northampton in England in 1899 by Wenman J. Bassett-Lowke. At the 1900 Paris Exhibition he met Stefan Bing, heralding the start of his long and close association with the German toy factories. Bassett-Lowke encouraged the Nuremberg companies to manufacture near-scale models, and to develop the smaller gauge items. Toy train products by Bing and Carette were initially 'anglicized' to Bassett-Lowke requirements. However, Bassett-Lowke later designed a series of locomotives and rolling stock which incorporated a number of basic standard parts, such as cylinders. It was this series of British-designed, German-built models which really established the Bassett-Lowke marque. The models were more faithful in both scale and detail to the trains they represented than those that the German factories had previously produced, and consequently W.J. Bassett-Lowke, who died in 1953, is today considered to be one of the founders of 'model' railways.

*Below: A Hornby No.2 Special Pullman Set comprising the clockwork 4-4-0 'County of Bedford' locomotive and six-wheel tender, and two bogie Pullman cars, 'Iolanthe' and 'Arcadia'. The set would have cost £3-5s-0d in the early 1930s.*

# TOY TRAINS

Ives and Lionel were both American companies whose products, along with those from Germany, tried to satisfy the huge U.S. market. The Ives Railway Lines company was founded in Plymouth, Connecticut by Edward Ives in 1886, moving to Bridgeport in 1874 as production of tinplate toys increased. In 1901 0-gauge railway sets were introduced, which were very successful in the early years, and they had electric sets in production by 1910. The early locomotives were constructed of cast iron, with rolling stock traditionally of printed tinplate. In 1904 Ives increased their range to include gauge 1, because Lionel had begun to concentrate its efforts on the 0-gauge. Edward Ives died in 1918, and later, like Bing, the Ives Company suffered badly during the 1920s' trade recession, resulting in the company being taken over and merged into the Lionel Corporation in 1930. By 1932 the famous name of Ives Railway Lines had vanished from the market.

The Lionel Corporation, Ives' major market competitor, was started by Joshua Lionel Cowen in New York as a retail shop in 1901. He had begun manufacturing toy train sets by 1908, and soon demand for Lionel toys had the company moving to a larger factory in Irvington, New Jersey. They concentrated on 0-gauge railway products, for which they became famous in Britain as well as in America. Lionel locomotives were very detailed and boasted impressive performance despite their heavy die-cast metal construction. Although not as attractive as some contemporary European products, they are nonetheless very handsome vehicles, being well made and robust. J.L. Cowen died in 1965 and in 1970 the Lionel name and manufacturing rights were leased to the Model Product Corporation.

Both Lionel and Ives products would have been comparatively expensive in Britain, and although quite rare they are not as highly rated among collectors as European products. Naturally the reverse applies to American collectors, where both marques are highly sought-after.

## AFTER 1914

After the assassination of the Archduke Franz Ferdinand when visiting Sarajevo, and resulting onset of the Great War, the European metal toymakers turn their factories over to manufacturing the products of war. Frank Hornby's Meccano factory at Binns Road, Liverpool, had restricted toy production because of the munitions work it was carrying out for the government. The proposed production of model railways had been shelved, and by 1918 'Meccano boys' were being informed by the Company that 'All our machines which are suitable are devoted to government work.' The end of World War I with the armistice of 1918, and the Treaty of Versailles which imposed harsh reparation terms upon Germany, ensured that the previously competitive German industries, in-

Above: *A good display of pre-World War II Marklin gauge '0' electric railway models including locomotives, passenger carriages, and goods wagons. c.1935.*

cluding toy manufacturers, were rendered ineffective in European trade. The immediate consequence was that British products had a competitive edge over those of Germany and Austria, which were shunned and loathed by Britannia and her empire. Meccano Ltd was already a major manufacturer of toys in Britain and so the government encouraged the company to take advantage of the new chances that were arising. By 1920 *Meccano Magazine* was able to announce that the factory was ready to produce clockwork trains to replace those that were previously imported from the Continent. The magazine reported, 'We are very proud of this fine clockwork train system, and it will be a great favourite amongst boys,' and later in the same year it even went so far as to warn the buying public that 'supplies of foreign-made trains have found their way into this country, and your only protection is to insist that what you buy has been actually made in this country.'

Despite the strength of public feeling against anything German, Frank Hornby realized that the long-term success of his trains was dependant on equalling or surpassing the standard of pre-war German toys. The 'Hornby Train' was not inexpensive; however, its quality and design turned it into an immediate best-seller, and it went on in various forms to dominate the toy train market of Great Britain and her Empire until the closure of the Binns Road Meccano factory in 1980. Hornby products are by far the most

# TOY TRAINS

Left: *Three well-detailed Marklin gauge '0' tinplate carriages, including Deutsche Reichsbahn luggage coach, 1941/0 Personenwagan, and 1942/0 Mitropa dining car. c.1935.*

Below: *Three impressive Marklin gauge '0' electric locomotives and tenders. They are 'models' as opposed to 'toys' and would have been expensive to purchase when new. They are equally desirable today. c.1935.*

collectable and popular toy train products in Britain, where they are still plentiful and where they were such an important part of so many childhoods.

The first Hornby Train was an all-metal clockwork 0-gauge four-wheel 0-4-0 locomotive and tender. Three liveries were available, with the locomotives finished in Great Northern green, Midland Railway red, or London and North Western black. The Meccano catalogue states that the trains were available in 'One size only . . . Each set contains Engine, Tender and one Truck, set of Rails, including a circle and two straights. The engine is fitted with reversing gear, brakes and regulators. Complete in strong attractive box. 27/6d each.' It was the 'British and Guaranteed' nature of the Hornby product, which dominated the toy train market for so many years between the Wars and afterwards, that made Hornby a universal name.

The 'Hornby Train' range expanded rapidly and became the most comprehensive model railway system ever produced. Hundreds of locomotives, tank engines, and Continental trains had been represented when 0-gauge production ceased in the late 1960s. From the humble four-wheel 0-4-0 No. 1 locomotive to the twelve-wheel 4-6-2 'Princess Elizabeth' locomotive, the range had included engines such as the 'Flying Scotsman' and 'Royal Scot', undoubtedly the most famous locomotives of the age. Finely detailed commercial vans, wagons and tankers were transfer-printed with contemporary freight product names such as Fyffes' Bananas, Cadbury's Chocolates, Shell

Below: *A Hornby gauge '0' tinplate clockwork M2 passenger train set, manufactured by Meccano of Liverpool. c.1935.*

Above: *Three magnificent British model locomotives for gauge '0' sets including a Bassett-Lowke 4-6-0 'King George V', a Bassett-Lowke 2-6-0 Southern Railways 866, and a clockwork Hornby 4-4-0 'County of Bedford'. c.1935.*

Motor Spirit, Trinidad Lake Asphalt, and Nestles' Milk 'richest in cream'. Passenger coaches were similarly well decorated and detailed with opening doors and celluloid windows, and included corridor coaches, Pullman coaches and saloon coaches, with appropriate lettering and often boasting corridor connections and corridor end plates. The range of rolling-stock was complemented by printed tinplate engine sheds, tunnels, stations, platforms, signal cabins, station staff, passengers, Hornby Train books, etc. The range was truly huge, and this is what makes the marque so accessible to the train collector today. The majority of Hornby products can be located and purchased easily and reasonably, and the collecting interest has led to the founding of the Hornby Railway Collectors Association. The H.R.C.A. publish a journal which is full of news and interest for the enthusiast, and is a valuable source of Hornby information with contributions from members both on 0-gauge and table-top Dublo.

Bassett-Lowke, after one of his trips to Germany, introduced the Bing 00-gauge miniature table railway set to Britain in 1921. It was scaled at 1/8 inch to 1 foot (4mm to 305m) and travelled on a 5/8 inch (16mm) track. Eleven boxed sets were offered for sale, costing between 5/- and 37/6. While not being an immediate success, they did bring model railways to the mass market for the first time by virtue of their extremely cheap price. A typical Bing table railway set of the period was made up of a tinplate clockwork six-wheel

2-4-0 tank engine, approximately 4 inches (100mm) in length, two passenger coaches, a guard's van, a station, a tunnel, four signals, two telegraph poles and a quantity of track. The introduction of this German-made model railway awakened interest in gauge 00 and encouraged other British makers, including Frank Hornby, to develop their products.

Later, in 1935, the Trix company, formed by Stefan Bing, his son Franz and their partners, produced a 00-gauge railway system. W.J. Bassett-Lowke was behind the idea of the Trix Twin Railway, and when Hitler's regime began to make life unpleasant for the Jews in Germany, Bassett-Lowke was able to arrange for Franz Bing and others to come and live in England. Eventually, the T.T.R. was produced in Northampton and became a tremendous success. In 1938 Hornby launched the famous Dublo trains series which they claimed to be 'The Perfect Table Railway'. Available with either electric or clockwork power, the Hornby Dublo train system became as successful as the other Meccano, Hornby, and Dinky products produced at the Binns Road Factory in Liverpool.

The 00-gauge scale products soon replaced the larger gauge items in popularity and in production effort, with Meccano producing the Hornby Dublo range up until the company's closure in 1980. Most Trix Twin Railways and Hornby Dublo products are easy to find today and are still fairly inexpensive. However, they are not as popular among collectors as the 0-gauge or 1-gauge trains, which probably keeps the prices down. This makes '00' train sets and railway accessories an ideal point from which to start a toy train collection today.

Above: *A Hornby Dublo electric tank goods Train set no. EDG7 produced by Meccano Ltd. c.1950.*

Left: *A fairly modern and quite amusing tinplate toy train system produced in Hungary.*

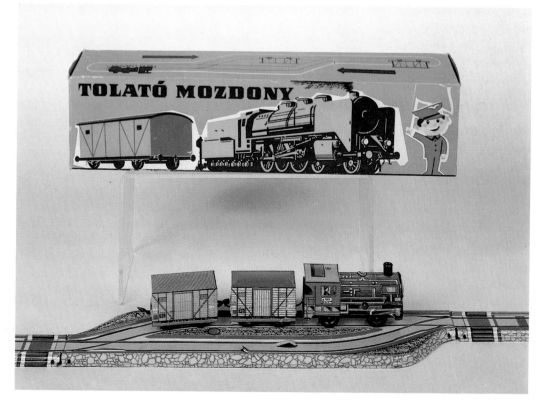

# TOY SOLDIERS
# AND FIGURES

*Miniature people and objects have always held*

*a fascination for children that is extended to the*

*adult collector. Of all the attempts by twentieth-*

*century toymakers to reduce the world to scale,*

*the toy figure is the most creative, and of these,*

*the archetypal figure has been the toy soldier.*

Deriving from a long tradition of figure-making going back to the funeral furniture of the Egyptian pharaohs, realistic miniature representations of people, their tools, animals and surroundings have been made. The most typical is the toy soldier, but more peaceful pursuits have also engaged the figure-makers, who have created a multitude of farms, zoos, circuses—covering in fact just about every activity that could stimulate the imagination of the growing mind; the last twenty years have seen an outburst of 'outer space' hero figures, from Buck Rogers to Dan Dare onwards.

The boundaries of a collection of figures are difficult to set, since many toys, such as model railways, cars, aircraft and so on, are often made with figures included. A certain amount of traditional definition has to be used to determine where one kind of toy stops and the other starts. For a child, the boundary is not so difficult, since the idea of using Dinky Toy army vehicles to back up an army of toy soldiers of a different scale is not disturbing. Only when we are adult does the striving for perfection drive us to make ever more realistic models, which then cease to be toys at all.

Because of the popularity of the toy soldier, nearly all figure-makers started by making these, and then added the other ranges at a later date. The important considerations have always been, on the one hand, mass production—to provide cheaply a large quantity of soldiers with which children can play their games—and on the other hand, realism—to delight the eye

*Left: Mignot 1st Empire. C.B.G. Mignot claims to be the earliest manufacturer of solid-cast toy soldiers in the world, tracing their history back to Revolutionary France through Lucotte. Napoleon is in the first row with his staff. The rifles and bayonets of these types of soldiers often become bent, and thus the whole group sold for £517 ($853) in 1988. Phillips London.*

Above: *Heyde historical figures. The German equivalent of the C.B.G. Mignot figures are these Heyde 45mm scale solid-cast soldiers showing the armies of Frederick the Great of Prussia, his allies and opponents at the time of the Seven Years War, c.1760. The actual figures were made c.1990. The total price of the collection shown was £3,333 ($5,500) in 1984. Phillips London.*

with beautifully formed figures, detailed uniforms, bright colours and steadfast facial expressions. Because of this breadth of purpose, there has been a constant supply of a bewildering variety of figures, from the most intricate (and expensive) to the meanest (often unpainted); from the full-dress panoply of ceremonial to the camouflage of the modern battle-field. It is from this great range of figures, added to each time science provides yet better ways of producing them, that today's collector can choose.

Toy soldiers look best *en masse*, and manufacturers have usually provided ranges at various constant scales, the most popular of which has been about 54mm (2⅙ inches) tall for a foot soldier. Toy soldiers and figures range in size from 20mm (¾ inch) to 100mm (4 inches), seldom smaller or larger, as the former become too small to see properly and the larger become more doll-like, such as a G.I. Joe or Action Man.

Which figures to collect can be decided by scale, manufacturer, subject or manufacturing process, but most collectors start by finding something that has particular appeal for them or that reminds them of something they had as a child. From then on the collection grows whenever something takes their fancy. Only when a fairly large collection has been amassed, say 500 to 1000 pieces, can it be sorted into themes and started on a more specialized course. Furthermore, toy figure collecting can be made to suit the pocket, since, like postage stamps, common examples are often worth less than one might think, while expensive sets run into thousands of pounds or dollars. A large collection of the products of one of the major manufacturers could comprise many thousands of toy figures, although not many collections are known to exceed 50,000 pieces.

Left: *Heyde Forage train, with steel helmets. Heyde No.2 size figures were about 45mm tall for foot figures, and often the horses were somewhat undersized for their riders. This interesting set is numbered 680 in its original box. The 680 is a reference to the components of the set, i.e. the Victualling column, and these might be found in a wide variety of other uniforms than the field grey with steel helmets that is depicted here. The column itself comprises open wagon, covered wagon and forage wagon, each with officer, two cavalry, cyclist and two dogs, with two seated guards on the forage wagon, a total of twenty-four pieces. The wagons themselves are made of tinplate, the figures of solid-cast lead alloy. The price of this set, at £242 ($400), was considerably lower than expected.*

Right: *East Kent Regiment in khaki. Only a few examples of this version of the East Kent Regiment are known to exist. It is thought that, at about the time of the Boer War of 1900, Britains painted set 16 in khaki uniform of the sort being used in South Africa. This set contains the normal drummer and bugler as well as seven on guard and the officer. In spite of some missing helmet spikes and bayonets, an original, unrepainted set of this type could be worth £1,000 ($1,650). Phillips London.*

Right: *East Kent Regiment. The East Kent Regiment was Britains' set 16, first made in 1894. This example contains just nine figures on guard and an officer. Conjecturally, the drummer and bugler that are normally included in this set were added later, after Britains brought out their Drums and Bugles set 30 in 1895. The box in which this set was originally sold is also shown, collectors much prizing the charming decorative style of the label. At this stage, Britains had not started to include the set numbers in the labels, which they did from 1898. This set was sold for £352 ($580) in 1988. Phillips London.*

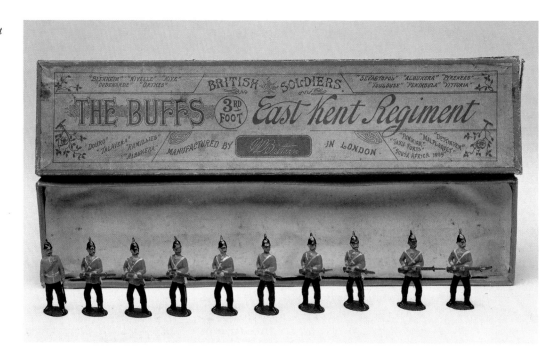

## A HISTORICAL SURVEY OF MANUFACTURE

At the turn of the century, four processes were in use for the production of toy figures:

### FLAT FIGURES

Made of tin alloy, these are two-dimensional silhouettes, showing the front and back of the item represented. Many are particularly finely engraved. The most common scale is about 30mm (1⅙ inches).

### SOLID FIGURES

Made of lead alloy, these are fully rounded figurines, cast solid, often with many parts soldered together. Sizes range from very small to very large, the most popular being between 45mm (1¾ inches) and 60mm (2⅓ inches). Some solid-cast figures were not fully three-dimensional, being about halfway between a solid and a flat. These are known as semi-flats.

### HOLLOWCAST FIGURES

Made of lead alloy, these are fully rounded, but with a hollow centre, requiring about half the metal of a solid to manufacture. Reputedly invented in 1893 by

William Britains, the process was soon taken up by other manufacturers. The most popular size was 54mm (2⅙ inches).

### COMPOSITION FIGURES

Also invented about the turn of the century, these were made of a wood, glue and plaster mixture that was moulded over a wire framework. The large size first issued was 100mm (4 inches), but the most popular size was later about 70mm (2⅔ inches).

Germany was in the forefront of manufacture, with France not far behind. Heinrichsen was the premier maker of flat figures, followed by Allgeyer and Haffner. At this time, flat figures were gradually being superseded as popular boy's toys by semi-flat and solid figures, leaving the flat figures as more a collectable for adults, as they still are today. Heyde and Heinrich were the premier manufacturers of solids, although both also began to produce hollowcast figures in response to the challenge from Britains.

In France, C.B.G. Mignot was the leading firm, their typical product being beautifully produced solid figures of 54mm (2⅙ inches), most often harking back to the Napoleonic Wars. Even more beautiful were the similar products of Lucotte. The two firms merged during the nineteenth century, although both ranges continued to be made. These solid figures are still the aristocrats of all toy soldiers, although a number of the German figures in similar or larger scales were equally as well made and painted. Mignot models are still being made today in a rather spasmodic fashion, and so are more frequently obtainable than their German counterparts.

British industry was mounting a challenge to what was previously an imported toy with the emergence of William Britains' native product, the hollowcast toy soldier. Produced by this firm from 1893 to 1966, and supplemented by many other English makers using the same process, such as Johillco, Reka, B.M.C., Crescent Timpo and Cherilea, hollowcast figures became the world's most widespread toy soldiers from 1990 to the 1950s, after which they were superseded by plastic products.

The process was taken up in many other countries, by manufacturers threatened by an influx of British imports, or, as in America, determined to 'do it cheaper' indigenously. Mignot in France was perhaps the firm who used the most different methods of production, as they brought out a large range of excellent flat figures, various hollowcasts, and aluminium and plastic items, as well as their top-of-the-line solids. Such was the internationalization of the toy industry that, for the period 1935 to 1950 in the USA, the most popular inexpensive toy soldiers made were by the hollowcast method, but in the 70-mm (2⅔-inch) scale usually associated with German

Above: *Mignot airfield. The C.B.G. Mignot Airfield display is typical of the interesting playsets with scenic backgrounds with which Henri Mignot revitalized the range from World War I onwards. Aircraft were the most exciting development of the early years of the 20th century. Phillips London.*

Above: *American Hero box. This set of Cowboys and Indians is typical of those issued by the American Soldier Company in New York from 1908 to about 1930. As here, the figures included were often supplied by Britains. The distinguishing feature of these sets, however, was the hinged tinplate clips into which the figures were fitted, which enabled them to be stood up on the baseboard and then, when knocked down with toy gunfire, to be stood up again with a quick turn of the board. The action can be observed in the Indian to the centre of the board which has been knocked over. A popgun was originally included in the box. This particular set was probably issued in the 1930s.*

Left: *Set 131 figures. Shown here are some of the unusual figures from Britains' largest ever set, the massive 275-piece set 131. At the back are two British Camel Corps as used in the Sudan, which only appeared in this set. If such a set came onto the market in good condition, it might well be worth £20,000 ($33,000). Phillips London.*

Right: *U.S. Cavalry specials. Britains were always open to offers for making special figures not in their catalogue. Some collectors, particularly during the 1930s, commissioned large numbers of special figures from them. These U.S. Cavalry are an example, being Boer Cavalry castings specially painted in a different uniform. These special paintings, if well authenticated, command high prices, and this set sold for £1,045 ($1,724) in 1988, over £200 ($330) each. The Indian figure which the cavalry are chasing is of unknown manufacture. It shows a typical Indian posture firing from beneath the neck of the horse, as seen in numberless western movies, but this is the only known example of a toy figure depicting this. The tail of the horse is broken off, but this is such a fascinating figure that it is well worth including in a collection, and might even be found very cheaply. Phillips London.*

Above: *Britains model fort: set 1394. This is one of the rarest of all Britains sets, since the cardboard fort that is included with the two-row box of soldiers is very fragile, easily destroyed and discarded. So very few have survived, that the price for this one in 1988 was £6,600 ($10,890). Phillips London.*

composition figures rather than the standard hollow-cast size an inch shorter. Prominent manufacturers included Barclay, Manoil and Grey Iron.

In the USA, with the notable exception of Warren (1936–39), there were no manufacturers producing toy figures of the quality of the best European products, which thus continued to be imported in considerable quantities. Because of this, the USA is now the world's leading centre of collecting for all types of toy soldiers, while in other countries the products of native firms predominate to the exclusion of most outsiders.

Also in contrast to other countries, the products of American makers catering to cheap toy outlets, the 'dimestores', are highly collectable, whereas second- or third-rate products of firms such as Britains or Mignot are rather spurned in England or France. So well regarded are the 'dime-store' figures that a great deal of trade in them has made them a distinct, separate and additional market to the mainstream of hollowcast collecting which centres around William Britains' range.

Composition figures, pioneered by the German firm of Hausser with the Elastolin range, became very popular in Germany during the 1920s and 1930s, culminating before World War II in a range of German army and Nazi Party figures unrivalled for their imaginative, all-embracing range of armed forces and political personalities. The rival German firm of Lineol produced a range similar to Elastolin, possibly even finer in execution, and there were a number of other companies in Germany, Austria, Italy and Belgium producing figures by this method, some surviving in the 1950s. Hausser's product also turned to plastic in the 1950s, where their artistry reached new heights in their many historical ranges. Now under new ownership, the plastic models of Hausser continue to be produced, and the old moulds of Lineol are also being used to revive some of the original range.

In the 1930s in France, a method of casting aluminium figures in sand was developed, and a range of 54-mm (2⅛-inch) figures was produced by Quiralu, Jouets Philippe and others as well as Mignot, who used the name Mignalu. Quiralu, who were the leading maker by this method, enjoyed some success with these figures into the early 1950s, their virtue being that they were virtually unbreakable. They even backed an English venture which went by the trade name Wend-Al, using many of their Quiralu moulds before designing more of their own.

Nevertheless, as far as toy soldiers for children

Left: *Barclay and Manoil medical figures. Examples of 3¾-inch scale Barclay and Manoil 'Dime Store' figures dating from the second half of the 1930s. Here displayed are medical personnel and wounded soldiers. Average individual figures from these manufacturers currently cost about $25 (£15) each in excellent condition, unless they are among the rarer items, in which case up to and over $1,000 (£606) has been known to change hands. This picture is from 'The Art of the Toy Soldier', courtesy of New Cavendish Books.*

Below: *Here are the comparatively rare number 623 Detective with pistol, worth about $80 (£48), and number 624 Burglar, worth about $60 (£36). This picture is from 'The Art of the Toy Soldier', courtesy of New Cavendish Books.*

were concerned, all the above methods of production were forced to give way to plastic injection moulding, which was introduced and developed from 1947 onwards. For the past thirty-five years, since about 1955, toy soldiers have been mainly made in plastic, and they have not been unworthy of their predecessors. Some of the early (pre-1960) makers' plastic products, such as those of the British firm Malleable Mouldings, have become very rare and sought-after, and the regular lines of the premier firms of the various nations are also highly collectable—Elastolin of Germany, Starlux of France, Herald and Britains of Britain, and Marx of the USA. In addition there are products of a host of other less well-regarded makers, many of whom converted from metal to plastic when the new technology became available. There was also a trend back toward providing children with large quantities of unpainted figures, since unlike metal toys, plastic was non-toxic, and also because the hand work required to paint the figures was becoming too expensive in comparison to mass-produced mouldings.

Left: *Warren figures. As can be seen here, Warren toy soldiers were of superior manufacture and finish. They purely portrayed the U.S. Army of the late 1930s when they were manufactured. Here are shown a magnificent group of cavalry with standards, a Warren speciality. They were expensive to purchase originally, and not very widely distributed, so, as rare and attractive items, the prices asked for them today are high, in the order of $150 (£91) each for cavalrymen, and up to double that for standard-bearers. This picture is from 'The Art of the Toy Soldier', courtesy of New Cavendish Books.*

Above: *King George VI wanted to see what his Life Guards would look like in an old pattern of helmet, and he asked Britains to make up a figure. It sold in 1989 for £1,210 ($1,996), and is the second most expensive single figure ever sold at auction— a figure of the Prince of Wales (later Edward VIII) sold for £1,320 ($2,178). Phillips London.*

Plastic was also responsible for the advent of a new generation of model kits, so that modelling and painting became one of the new hobbies of the 1960s. The idea of painting one's own toys became popular, and gradually the firms producing cheaper painted products were squeezed out of business, in spite of many ingenious attempts to assemble plastic figures from pre-coloured parts. The current production Elastolin 70-mm (2⅔-inch) figures imported fully painted from Germany are on sale at over £5 ($8) each.

Yet even as the advent of plastic was causing the end of metal production at the cheap end of the market, new centrifugal moulding techniques were giving a new lease of life to the quality end. As collectors of metal figures began to boost the prices of old figures in the 1970s, so a new style of solid-cast figure made its appearance, designed in the style of the old toy figure, and intended to take its place alongside the toys previously meant for children, which have now become adult collectables. The variety of these new toy soldiers is no less than the old; in fact, because of the new casting machines that allow short runs, there are probably more different models among the new than there ever were among the old. Seeing the new market, some of the previously established toy and model companies have joined in to cater for it, notably Alymer of Spain, Tradition of England, and Mignot of France. It should also be noted that the solid-cast figure had made an early brief resurgence through the US firm of Comet, with their Authenticast line made in Ireland, whose products were widely marketed

in the USA around 1948.

Britains in England has taken a different route, by developing a new die-cast technique that allows figures to be cast off automatically using cheaper zinc alloy, as used for die-cast cars. They are now producing a series of sets for collectors, and have recently re-issued figures that they first produced experimentally in die-cast form over 40 years ago. The irony is that until the re-issued figures were on offer, the original ones were not much sought-after by collectors, selling for just £1–2 ($2–3) each. The new sets on offer, however, price individual figures at about £3 ($5) each.

The methods of manufacture above do not by any means exhaust the ways in which toy soldiers have been made—tinplate, cardboard, wood, paper and plaster are some of the other media used. However, the methods and makers above comprise the mainstream of the collectable product, even if there are many hundreds of lesser makers unmentioned.

## IDENTIFYING MANUFACTURERS

Because toy soldiers are meant to be displayed in large numbers together, there is a tendency to collect those of a particular scale or manufacturer. Among the various makers there are many wildly differing styles of sculpture and painting, which do not always stand happily together. With other lead figures, the mass effect is not so important, and many charming vignettes can be made up with just a few figures. On the other hand, some manufacturers such as Britains made so many accessories, for instance the miniature garden, that by adding these together to form nearly lifelike scenes, a most satisfying amalgam can be obtained.

Identifying manufacturers can be a problem if the name is not readily visible underneath the base of the figure. Some makers were quite adept at hiding names or trademarks in unlikely places, but usually, if it is not easily seen, the name is not there at all. Then it is a matter of matching the style of the figure to a likely maker, although a definite attribution cannot be made until a reference in a catalogue can be found. Since manufacturers did not catalogue their product, or the catalogues have been lost, the history of many figures remains unknown.

## COLLECTABLE TOY FIGURES

The products of the British firms Charbens and Taylor & Barrett are widely collected because of the fine detail and imagination that went into the models, which nonetheless retained their toylike quality. Charbens are famous for their series of horse-drawn vehicles: the coal cart, with sacks of coal, and the coalmen carrying one; the brewer's dray, with six barrels of beer and the ladder down which they are made to roll on their journey to the innkeeper's cellar; and the tar boiler with its chimney, that can be added to the road-mending set, to name but three examples. Taylor & Barrett produced costermongers with their barrows

Left: *Elizabeth Coronation set. Britains set 2081, the largest set of toy soldiers made by Britains after World War II. It contained 228 figures, and depicted the coronation procession of Queen Elizabeth II. It was only available from Britains in 1953, and never seems to have appeared in the catalogue. Although this is a very large set of soldiers, the figures of which it is composed are not rare, and so the expected price for a complete boxed set would be about £3,000 ($4,950), or only just over £13 ($21) per figure, which is about what the individual figure components of the set are worth. Phillips London.*

Below: *Cherilea baseball set. This Cherilea baseball team is a most exciting example, since very few specifically American non-military sets were made. This would in all probability be worth between £500 ($825) and £1,000 ($1,650) should it be on offer in 1990, but it is so rare that it could be worth more. This picture is from 'The Art of the Toy Soldier', courtesy of New Cavendish Books.*

selling vegetables—onions, cauliflowers and marrows separately moulded—or cats in baskets with kittens so small they would be lost if they ever left their mother's side.

Britains produced their first civilian figures when they made football teams in 1904. Non-military lead figures became much more widespread after World War I when military toys fell into disfavour. These themes now form the bases of many intriguing collections: farms, zoos, hunts, circuses, Boy Scouts, the Salvation Army, railway personnel and passengers, police, workmen, tradespeople, firemen, dancers and sportsmen.

The effect of the cinema was also seen quite early on with the appearance of cowboys and Indians before World War I. Later, particularly in the 1950s, there was to be a flowering of figures representing all the romantic, historical cinema and television themes such as the French Foreign Legion, Arabs, Robin Hood, pirates, knights in armour and Romans. Many of the plastic playsets made by Marx were linked to specific television programmes, and this type of character merchandize extended to children's TV cartoons, comic paper characters, nursery rhymes and so on, in a surprisingly wide variety.

The attraction of many of these figures is that they are readily recognizable, and have a story to tell. The value of figures is often a complex relationship between their availability, attractive appearance, and the number of different collections that they readily fit into. The highlights of a collection of Britains toy soldiers for adults are more often the superb full-dress cavalry, Highlanders, military bands or horse-drawn artillery. For their original young customers, action poses were

more popular, particularly in the cheaper lower grades. Footguards were always a good selling line, and so are quite easily found today.

For those willing to spend time and artistry restoring broken figures, this is an excellent way of achieving a mass effect on a low budget. This perfectly legitimate practice does, however, sometimes lead the unwary purchaser into expensive mistakes when buying something purporting to be in original condition when it is in fact restored. Original hollowcast figures are considerably lighter than their re-cast replicas, but this difference will not be noticeable when there is just a small repair. Careful examination of the paintwork and a good familiarity with paint style, tone, colour and texture are the best ways round this difficulty. Above all, a good toy figure collection should be a great display of colourful pageantry and history, as well as an authentic social record in miniature.

# DIE-CAST TOYS

*The die-cast toy, usually found in the form of*

*cars, commercial and military vehicles, racers*

*and aircraft, is probably the most prolific toy of*

*our age, and there are more collectors in this*

*field than in any other.*

The typical die-cast toy is a model car made of metal. It is, according to its age, made of one or more castings, and is put together with chassis, baseplate, axles, wheels, welds and screws, possibly with plastic or plated accessories. The vast majority of boys who have grown up during the last 40 years had drawers full of them. Apart from the fun of re-creating in good condition the collection that was destroyed as a child, the adult collector has an amazing variety from which to choose. The favourite ways to collect are by specific manufacturer, or by type of vehicle.

The major manufacturers' trademark lines with a sufficient range to form a fair-sized collection from:

**Britain:** Dinky, Corgi, Matchbox, Britains, Spot-On, Lledo
**USA:** Tootsietoy, Mattel Hot Wheels, Ertl
**Denmark:** Tekno
**France:** C.I.J. Europarc, Majorette, Solido, Dinky France
**Germany:** Gama, Siku
**Italy:** Burago, Polistil, Mercury, Rio
**Japan:** Dandy, Diapet

Some of these manufacturers produced so many toys that a good collection can be made from just sections of their production. A typical example would be the Matchbox Yesteryear series with over 100 models, not counting the many different variations and liveries in which these models of veteran and classic vehicles have appeared.

The favourite types of vehicle to collect are road

cars, by marque, type—i.e., small, luxury, sports, veteran or classic—commercial vehicles by marque, purpose—i.e., military, agricultural, firefighting, construction, railway-related, road haulage, buses, taxis, police, rescue and emergency—or off-road racing cars by marque or sport, bikes, record cars, or special vehicles. In a collection of this nature, many of the smaller manufacturers can feature, some of whose models are extremely rare.

Vehicles can also be collected by scale, since for an adult it is satisfying to have all models correctly related to one another in a way that toy manufacturers and children do not worry about overmuch. Die-cast vehicles in their early days were not particularly accurate models, and tended to be near 1/48 scale; larger vehicles would be usually portrayed in smaller scales. In the 1950s, most model cars were produced around 1/43 scale, with Matchbox toy cars being about 1/72 scale. In the 1960s to 1980s, scales tended to increase, primarily to accommodate special features and give better value.

Die-cast toys can also be collected generically by method of manufacture or period of manufacture, in order to illustrate their history, marketing or packaging, or collected as toys rather than models. Particularly since 1965, character merchandizing has formed a large part of the output of toys (see Chapter on T.V.

Right: *The Dinky Lyons Swiss Roll van sold for £1,870 ($3,086) at Phillips London in 1988. The transfer decals of the advertisements on the sides are relatively fragile, and the price reduces dramatically if these have been damaged.*

Toys) and special play features such as low-friction wheels, science fiction versions such as Transformers, and a tendency towards novelty and fantasy in vehicles designed to attract younger children, have been the major recent directions. In contrast, models have been made more with the adult collector in mind.

However, die-cast toys have by no means been limited to vehicles, and ranges of aircraft, ships, trains, toy soldiers, even doll's house furniture, have been made.

## EARLY DAYS AND THE ADVENT OF DINKY, 1900–1954

The earliest die-cast toys may be from a manufacturer in France, Simon & Rivolet, who marked their products S.R. These were made in intricate moulds using lead alloy, often with parts made of tinplate, many of them quite charming and in small sizes. S.R. also

manufactured toy guns and vehicles to go with the C.B.G. Mignot range of toy soldiers. The range was well established by 1905, and competed with the tinplate 'pennytoys'.

The earliest US die-cast toys are credited to Samuel Dowst, a Chicago trade journal publisher who had the bright idea of adapting a linotype typecasting machine to make all sorts of other miniature castings. By 1911 he produced what was to be the first of a famous line of toy vehicles, a small limousine 47mm (1⅘ inches). Some of the toys he produced are very similar to S.R., from whose products he may have got the idea. In 1922, he produced some doll's house furniture under the trade name Tootsietoy, derived from a relative's daughter named Tootsie, and this trade name proved so popular and memorable that the whole line of toys moved under this banner.

Many of the themes evident in the later plethora of die-cast toys are evident in this pioneering line, including the use of logos, with for instance, J.C. Penny on the sides of commercial vehicles, character merchandize based on popular comic-paper characters of the time such as 'Uncle Walt Wallet', cars, aircraft,

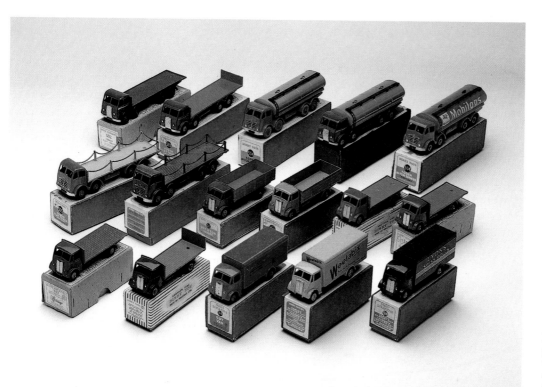

Above: *In 1988 a near complete collection of Dinky Toys was sold at Phillips London, and this and the following pictures show an interesting cross-section of what a major collection of Dinky Toys should contain. Top left is the most famous boxed set of all, set 22 motor vehicles, the first vehicle set ever issued. This sold for £2,200 ($3,630). The five 23c Mercedes Benz racing cars in their half-dozen trade box, top right, sold for £1,210 ($1,996). Two differently coloured sets 24, of motor cars, came next, selling for £3,300 ($5,445) and £5,500 ($9,075) respectively. This set went through numerous variations of mould and colour during its six-year life, and collectors are intrigued by the intricacies of these.*

Left: *Dinky commercials. This picture shows the larger commercial vehicles of the 1950s. The most sought-after are the 514 series Guy vans with advertisements on the sides.*

# DIE-CAST TOYS

Right: *Dinky buses. Buses are one of the most popular themes for collectors, and as can be seen in this picture, Dinky made many different models. Prices ranged from £50 to £100 ($80 to $165) for each boxed bus, but the Post Office services gift set 299 was sold for £660 ($1,089).*

Below: *Dinky racing cars. Recalling the great racing names of the 1950s, the roll reads, top to bottom, left to right: 230 Talbot Lago; 231 Maserati; 232 Alfa Romeo; 233 Cooper Bristol; 234 Ferrari; 235 HWM; 236 Connaught; 237 Mercedes Benz (two); 238 Jaguar D Type, and 239 Vanwall.*

military vehicles, and so on. Although early models were made in lead alloy, by the late 1920s the zinc alloy called mazac or zamac had been introduced. Mazac will not run through a mould in the same way as lead, and so has to be pressure-injected. This is the basic method of making die-cast toys that has remained standard ever since, although the casting machinery has been constantly improved.

Exports from both these ranges soon arrived on the British toy market, where nothing comparable was yet being made. Frank Hornby, the inventor of Meccano and manufacturer of Hornby trains, in 1931 had the idea of 'Modelled Miniatures', the first being figures to go with his 0-gauge railways. In 1934, Set 22 of this series contained the first road vehicles—a sports car, a sports coupe, a motor truck, a delivery van, a farm tractor and an army tank. Although these were all marked 'Hornby Series', they mark the beginning of the most famous line of die-cast toys, christened 'Dinky Toys' later in 1934, destined to become the most desirable collector's toys of today. An explosion of inventive production took place during that same

year, adding more vehicles, aeroplanes and ships to the already existing figures and play-trains. By the end of the year, advertizing could claim '150 Varieties' in emulation of a famous food producer.

From the first, as promoted in the *Meccano Magazine*, this was a new hobby for children—'Collecting Meccano Dinky Toys'—and by 1938 there were over 300 toys in the range. Until after World War II, there was no noticeable competition to this outpouring of product. Children in Britain and overseas were embracing the new realistic toys as fast as they could

Below: *Dinky Toy 28 series delivery vans. Twenty-five were on sale on this occasion, the most popular proving to be 28m, Wakefield Castrol Motor Oil, and 28n Meccano (first type), which sold for £1,430 ($2,359) each, and the least popular 28r, Swan Pens, which sold for £352 ($581).*

Below: *Various early Dinky aircraft. The yellow trade box of six low-wing monoplanes 60d sold for £374 ($617). Because of metal fatigue, the 62p Armstrong Whitworth Ensign Air Liner, top left, only sold for £50 ($82). The Mayo Composite Aircraft with the seaplane embarked, is one of the most extraordinary aircraft made, set 63, and sold for £242 ($399) in spite of fatigue.*

Above: *An early French Dinky box for aircraft with beautiful period graphics.*

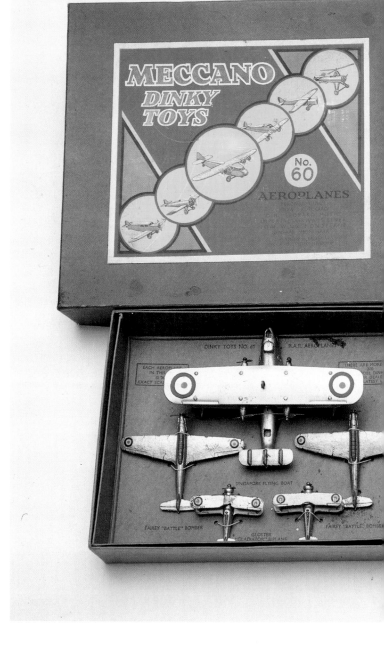

Above: *Dinky aircraft were a major feature of the range from early on, and form a fascinating collection in their own right. The 1930 to 1960 period was that in which aviation was developing fastest in every conceivable direction, so that the toys mirror the most exciting era of aviation history.*

be produced. Sooner or later, competition was bound to emerge, but because of war and subsequent shortages of metal, this was not to be until the 1950s.

## COMPETITION IN THE BRITISH AND EXPORT MARKETS, 1954–1968

Competition eventually arrived in the shape of Matchbox Toys, which in 1954 improved on the Dinky idea by making them smaller, and then in 1956 with Corgi Toys, who used the new technology of plastic to add features such as windows. Other European nations were also starting ranges, notably those of Gama and Siku in West Germany, Tekno in Denmark, Solido in France, and Mercury in Italy. The USA remained the best export market, but the market was now really a battle between three giant British makers—Dinky, Corgi and Matchbox—with all the early rounds going to the newcomers as a result of a continuing programme of innovation in which Dinky was left far behind. In 1964, Meccano, including Dinky Toys, was taken over by Lines Brothers, in the first of a succession of re-organizations of the British and then the international toy industry that has been such a feature of the past three decades.

The two relative newcomers took up all the running in the burgeoning market for British-made die-cast toys, an age that lasted from 1952, when the end of the Korean War lifted the restriction on the supply of zinc, until the American marketing counter-attack based on low-friction wheels, spearheaded by Mattel with their 'Hot Wheels', in 1968.

Corgi Toys were introduced, from 1956, with an increasing host of features new to die-cast in their toys: windows, spring suspension, opening bonnet and detailed engine, self-centering steering, opening boot/trunk, jewelled headlamps and ruby rear lights,

even working windscreen wipers. In the battle for sales, ever more intricate extras were included. By 1963, Corgi had produced their number 241, the Ghia L.6.4., with opening doors, bonnet/hood and boot/trunk, jewelled front and rear lights, plated chrome parts, tip-up seats, detailed dashboard and driving mirror, a Corgi dog passenger, and spring suspension—in all, twelve features for a car which in real life was only sold to six people, but as a model sold to one and three quarter million.

In 1965, Corgi started producing character merchandize. Their first toy was TV-related, the Saint's Volvo, but the surprising success was the second, the

# DIE-CAST TOYS

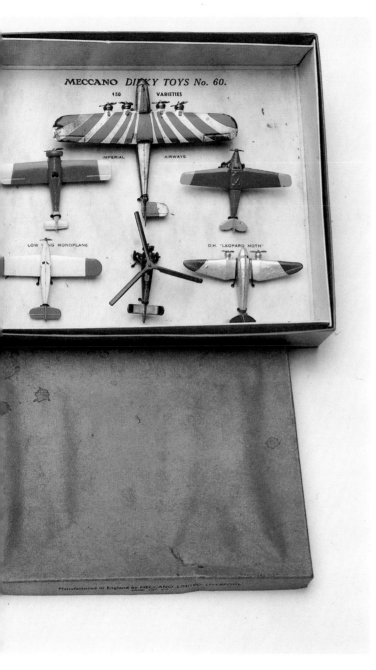

scale Minic ships, the only extensive range produced in die-cast. Dinky had produced some in 1/1800 before the War, but the models of other major manufacturers, Wiking and Treforest Mouldings, had been produced in lead alloy. Both Mercury and Wiking later produced die-cast models.

Lines Brothers made a later entry into the die-cast toy vehicle market in 1959 with the introduction of their Spot-On range. The idea was to produce slightly larger vehicles than the normal Dinky or Corgi models, in 1/42 scale, and to ensure a very high and consistent quality of windows, accessories and finish, with particular emphasis on all the vehicles being strictly in scale with each other. It was particularly noticeable that their commercial vehicles were much larger than those of their competitors, who tended to reduce the scale for these. For this reason, Spot-On lorries are much sought-after by collectors, although at the time it meant that they were expensive to buy.

Also in the Spot-On range were accessories such as the Cotswold Village made of moulded rubber, the roadway, signs and garages, and the Arkitex building system. Between them, these accessories made up a townscape more realistic than anything previously attempted for model vehicles. Although only the vehicles were die-cast toys, the complete Spot-On collection is visually extremely interesting and attractive as a record of 1950s' architecture as well as vehicles.

Sadly, because of its expense, the Spot-On range, made in Northern Ireland, did not make a major impact on the market. Once Lines Brothers had taken over Meccano with its Dinky Toys in 1964, they lost interest in developing the Spot-On range further. From 1968, production was transferred to New Zealand to take advantage of the closed market there.

Play value was very evident in the items produced by Lesney Products starting in 1953. Leslie Smith and Jack Odell were northeast London toymakers in the

James Bond Aston Martin, with its ejector seat, hidden machine guns and pop-up bulletproof screen, as featured in the film *Goldfinger*. Over four million of this model were to be sold over five years, with the first year's supply being totally unable to keep up with the demand.

This was the first 'missile-firing' Corgi toy, although in this case the 'missile' was a bad guy being ejected. From now on, realism would more often be sacrificed to play value, as more and more gimmicky character merchandize and cartoon toys made their appearance. The Batmobile produced in 1966 was based entirely on the TV series fantasy vehicle.

Lines Brothers, with their Tri-Ang trademark, had been a large toy manufacturer since the 1920s, and included the Minic range of toy vehicles made first in tinplate and then in plastic. Their first major essay in die-cast toys was in 1958 with their range of 1/1200-

Below: *A highly attractive group of Marklin cars.*

# DIE-CAST TOYS

Right: *A beautiful group of colourful and mainly well preserved early cars.*

tradition of the area. Being versed in the methods of die-casting, and wanting to set up in business for themselves, they decided to try and make die-cast toys cheaper than Dinky Toys, to sell through the whole-sale trade. After a slow start, success came with the production of large and small coronation coaches in advance of the 1953 coronation of Queen Elizabeth II. Over a million of the small coaches were sold, and this gave the capital to start Matchbox Toys. The idea of these was a small die-cast toy, about 50mm (2 inches) long, that would fit in a matchbox-sized box, a complete toy at a very low cost. Unsuccessful in the 1953 Christmas season, sales of the first four small castings took off as pocket-money toys in the spring.

The first models were all commercial vehicles; number 19, the MG TD sports car, was the first car, released three years later in 1956. By 1960, the Match-box range had reached the 75 models that became standard, since at this level new releases could always be found a slot where a previous model had come to end of its commercial life. In addition to the standard range, from 1956, Lesney produced the Yesteryear

*Above: Marklin racing cars.*

series, a series that is probably more collected than any other range of toys worldwide, since from the start it appealed to adults as well as children.

Matchbox Toys benefitted from the continuing trend towards smaller scales in toys, and the growth of the zero-scale railway modelling boom of the 1950s. Many of the toys were of the right size to be scenic accessories, and could be promoted as such. Lesney also produced 'Major' packs and king-size models that were larger than Matchbox scale and which competed with Dinky and Corgi toys.

Many other small British makers previously inter-ested in toy figures and models began to produce die-casts, particularly Benbros, Morestone with 'Budgie Toys', Charbens, Crescent, and Lone Star with 'Road Masters' and 'Impy'. Most of these makers tried to compete with Dinky in one scale and with Matchbox in smaller sizes, usually on the basis of lower prices,

74

*Above: More Guy vans appear in this group, but these, being later issues, are not very expensive. Interestingly, the two sets of road signs are quite expensive at £462 ($762) for the two boxes. An unboxed Britains set of road signs sold in 1990 for £550 ($908).*

but although between them they produced some hundreds of models, none were particularly successful. Lone Star produced for a time an interesting range of 000-scale railways, with even the tracks being made of die-castings.

Britains, the toy soldier and figure manufacturers, started to use die-casting extensively in their range of guns and army vehicles, bicycles, motorbikes, and, most successfully, agricultural equipment. All of these were designed in 1/32 scale to complement the figures already produced. Eventually, after early experimentation, a range of die-cast toy soldiers was developed, which is now continuing to be increased.

In 1967 the British die-cast toy industry was at its peak. Lesney, employing 6,500, had a turnover of £28 million ($45,000,000), and was producing 5½ million Matchbox models a week. Mettoy, employing 3,000 to make Corgi toys, produced 17½ models that year. Reckoning that six Matchbox toys equal one Corgi toy in value, this shows Lesney outproducing Mettoy by about four to one in value and twenty-four to one in volume. Dinky Toys had already gone into a

decline, and was probably producing a considerably lesser quantity of toys by this stage.

### THE MODERN DIE-CAST SCENE

A major watershed in the production of die-cast toys arrived in 1968, when Mattel in the USA launched their new range of 'Hot Wheels'. This featured low-friction wheels and axles that enabled a car to be sent a much further distance with a single push, and with the addition of plastic track that gave the models all the fun of a speedway. So fickle is the toy industry that Hot Wheels soon wiped out over three-quarters of Matchbox sales. Mattel launched into Britain in 1969, and Matchbox were forced to introduce their own Superfast range to stay in business. Corgi fitted Whizzwheels to their cars, and Dinky, the slowest to react, had nonetheless introduced their Speedwheels by June 1969.

Not only were the new Mattel matchbox-sized cars fast, they and their competitors were soon also given garish colours and fantastic accessories borrowed from drag racing. Adult collectors were not impressed, but children loved them. One of the features of previous die-cast toys had been that they were so sturdily built that they effectively lasted forever. The new thin axles necessary for Hot Wheels would easily bend if the car was trodden on, and so a major replacement market

Above: *A highly attractive group of toys, showing the superb range available both for the generalist or for those who want to develop a speciality.*

Left: *One post-war aircraft has become legend, the limited production number 992 Avro Vulcan Delta Wing Bomber. It is possible that as few as 500 were made, and certainly the model is unique in that it is die-cast from aluminium rather than mazac, which led to difficulties so severe that production had to be halted. Genuine models in original condition are worth in excess of £1,000 ($1,650). Phillips London.*

was introduced that had not before existed. Mattel had their cars produced in the Far East, and this also proved to be a trend, as even the best automatic machinery developed by the British companies proved unable to keep costs down to the levels achieved in Hong Kong.

The short time in which the changeover to the new low-friction wheel system took place in a competitive market means that there were many models that had only a very short life on sale, and so are very difficult for collectors to find today. For Matchbox collectors, many of these models are more readily available in the USA, since the bulk of production was sold there, and the new models were released there first.

As with many good innovations, the new wheels actually increased the market for die-cast toys overall, and Lesney's Matchbox Toys, after converting, were soon selling more than ever alongside Mattel. By 1982, however, high costs and the British recession forced Lesney into liquidation. The company was bought by a Hong Kong company that has since been renamed Universal Matchbox and has since also acquired the Dinky trademark. With most of its production facilities in the Far East, this company is by far the largest producer of die-cast toys today, participating both in the general toy and the collector markets.

Jack Odell, after bowing out from Lesney, founded his own firm, Lledo, and has for some years been

producing a range of toys similar to the Yesteryear series. He is now the only major British-owned producer, since Corgi have been recently bought by Mattel. The market for die-cast toys has today polarized between models produced with collectors and older children in mind, and action toys for children of between five and ten, good modern examples of which are the Transformers—fantasy robots that transform into vehicles in order to undertake missions on earth. Character merchandize is also still much in vogue; for instance, one of the newer makers on the mass market scene, Ertl, which started with a small range of agricultural tractors, now sells die-cast models of Batman vehicles and the English children's train character Thomas the Tank Engine and his friends, among many others.

Many smaller makers cater to the collecting market, such as Exclusive First Editions with their range of commercial vehicles and buses. The major companies also produce limited editions and gift sets. The number of die-cast toys and models available continues to increase in direct proportion to the number of collectors. This ensures that making a complete collection of die-cast toys remains a virtual impossibility. Even keeping track of all the various products is difficult, and will doubtless provide fruitful fields of research in the future of this most prolific of toys.

Above: *A very handsome pair: a blue OXO delivery van, and a distinctive yellow and red Heinz delivery van.*

Below: *More commercial vehicles from Marklin, proving that functional everyday vehicles can be converted into wonderful toys just as readily as their more charismatic leisure and racing counterparts.*

Below: *A group of assorted die-cast toys.*

# T.V. TOYS

*T.V. and media toys are probably the fastest growing sector of the toy market, and since they involve most types of toy, they deserve a special consideration.*

Many potential toy collectors remark that, while being interested in toys, they find it hard to relate to antique or pre-war toys, and that their interests lie in the contemporary film, television and other media-inspired toys about which little information is available.

Media-influenced toys are normally cheaply produced and designed to cash in on what usually is a short-term fad or craze. They are based upon a familiar character or popular hero or even a villainous 'public enemy number-one' type character that has become popular with children through a television programme, current successful film or within the pages of the latest 'in' comic. The metamorphosis of media character into media character toy was once an interest peculiar to the Americans, because of the huge popularity of the cartoon character and the newspaper strip within their society during the 1920s and 1930s. However, like most things American, the influence soon spread to Britain and Europe.

Cartoon characters like Popeye the Sailorman began life as a newspaper strip in the 1930s, after which he appeared in many animated movies, and today he can still be seen on television. Popeye and many other characters, including the hugely successful creations of the Walt Disney Studios, have more or less stood the test of time and remained popular all over the world, thanks to a combination of marketing and continued influence. Consequently, the associated media toy merchandize is equally widespread around the world, with local toy producers satisfying the local demand for toy Batmans, Mickey Mouses, Darth Vaders, etc. It would not be unusual to discover a toy spinach-guzzling Popeye, on board a battery-powered

plastic boat, singing 'I'm Popeye the Sailorman' in Spanish.

Go into most toy shops and it is easy to see that Popeye and Mickey Mouse toys are just as popular as

Above: *A Dean's soft toy Mickey Mouse produced in England, c.1930. Standing a mere 5¾ins (15cms) tall, he is made of velvet and felt.*

Right: *Distler's Mickey Mouse Organ-Grinder, produced in Germany c.1930, shows Minnie Mouse dancing. 8ins (20cms) high, and 6ins (15.5cms) long.*

Right: *This Mickey Mouse Bagatelle game produced in England by the Chad Valley Co. Ltd, is colourfully printed. c.1950, 24ins × 12¼ins (61cms x 30.5cms).*

Far right: *A Louis Marx and Co. Ltd plastic climbing Popeye toy, produced in 1974, and proving that Popeye is just as popular as ever! Made in Hong Kong.*

ever. At the same time other media toys will be equally prominent on the shelves, such as Postman Pat, Thomas the Tank Engine, Ghostbusters, Batman, and Care Bears. Some, such as Postman Pat and Thomas the Tank Engine, are very British, and it is unlikely that the bright blue Hornby clockwork Thomas the Tank Engine train set will be available in toy shops in America or Japan. Similarly, it would be strange to find a red plastic toy Postman Pat and delivery van on sale in Spain.

The 1989 Batman film influenced a plethora of associated toy merchandize, mostly cheap and nasty, to cash in on the much-hyped return of D.C. Comic's famous caped crusader. Nevertheless it is likely that within a few years these pretty unimpressive plastic products, including the Batman, the Joker, Bob the Joker's Goon, the Batmobile, Batwing and the Batcave, will become collectable. Similarly, Steven Spielberg's Star Wars films of the 1970s provoked many mass-produced, low-quality associated toy products, which are collectable today. Because the interest in media toys is now so great, younger collectors are purchasing contemporary examples as soon as they appear in the shops.

Mickey Mouse is probably the best-known and most

Right: *Two examples of the James Bond Aston Martin DB5 Corgi toy produced by the Mettoy Company between 1965-1968, showing packaging and working features. 3¾ins (10cms).*

widely exploited example of a popular character who has been represented in nearly all types of merchandize. He has appealed to both sexes and all age groups for over 60 years, and is still as popular as ever. As early as 1930 Johann Distler of Nuremberg in Germany produced a very clever tinplate clockwork Mickey Mouse 'Organ Grinder' with a dancing Minnie. The clockwork mechanism operates Mickey's arm and a small musical movement within the organ. Unlike many character toys, which, after the novelty of the familiar character has worn off, the toy is found to be functionally disappointing, the Distler Mickey Mouse Organ Grinder is a very pleasing toy. It is brightly coloured and decorated with lithographs depicting Mickey and Minnie in humorous, musical situations. This particular toy is very highly prized by both collectors of tinplate and media toys, with examples fetching several hundreds of pounds or dollars in recent years.

Most character toys, irrespective of the period of manufacture, should display a copyright sign somewhere on the outer surface of the article, or on its sales box or packaging. So, officially authorized toy Popeye products on the market, for example, should carry a copyright sign for King Features Syndicate, while Mickey Mouse and Co. are obviously copyright of Walt Disney Productions of Walt Disney-Mickey Mouse Ltd. Unofficial media or character toys will usually not carry a copyright at all and will often be of

inferior quality; nonetheless, such toys are rare and therefore remain sought-after by collectors.

Although the interest in collecting Disney-related toys is mainly an American preoccupation, it is becoming increasingly popular in Britain and Europe, thus causing values for locally produced examples to increase fairly rapidly. In Britain it is the television-related toys that are amongst the most eagerly collected. T.V. programmes with a nostalgic or an effective appreciation society are usually the most popular, whether imported or locally produced, and with science fiction, cops and robbers, and pop music-related programmes being the most popular. Dr Who and the Daleks, Thunderbirds, Captain Scarlet, Joe 90, Star Trek, Kojak, The Man from U.N.C.L.E., James Bond, The Saint, The Avengers, Starsky and

Hutch, Batman and Robin, the Monkees and The Beatles, together with other familiar childhood friends and heroes including Noddy and Big-Ears, The Magic Roundabout, and Chitty-Chitty-Bang-Bang, have all been produced as toys in England under the ubiquitous Dinky and Corgi trademarks. Dinky toys, manufactured by Meccano Ltd. in Liverpool, and Corgi, manufactured by Mettoy Playthings of London, are more well-known for their comprehensive range of die-cast metal toy vehicles, ships and aeroplanes, and their T.V. and film-related models are unexpected an but exciting additional range.

The die-cast metal media toy products of the Dinky and Corgi ranges are fairly evenly divided between British and American subjects. Dinky were inspired by Gerry Anderson's clever futuristic adventure tele-

*Right: A group of Palitoy's Planet of the Ape range seen in action, exemplifying the great popularity of TV-related and promoted toys in the 1970s, '80s and '90s.*

*Below: Some 'Screen Favourites' from an earlier Corgi Toys catalogue, including Batman, James Bond, Chitty Chitty Bang Bang, and Daktari toys.*

270 James Bond Aston Martin DB5  4" 102mm
© 1967 Glidrose Productions Ltd. & Eon Productions Ltd.

## Screen Favourites

266 Chitty Chitty Bang Bang
Wings flick out at a touch of the brake lever — detachable front and rear fins — detachable figures — fantasmagorical detail!
© 1967 Glidrose Productions Ltd. & Warfield Productions Ltd.

GIFT SET No. 3 Batman's Batmobile and Batboat. Available separately:
107 Batboat on Trailer  5¼" 133mm
267 Batmobile  5½" 140mm
© National Periodical Publications Inc. 1966

26

GIFT SET No. 7 'Daktari' Gift Set

GIFT SET No. 14 Giant 'Daktari' Gift Set
From the world-wide television series about a scientist dedicated to preserving African wildlife. 'Daktari' means Doctor in Swahili.
© Ivan Tors Film Inc. Ltd. 1967

27

vision series, including Thunderbirds, Joe 90 and Captain Scarlet. Imaginative and very enjoyable working models of Lady Penelope's FAB 1, Thunderbirds 2 and 4, Joe's car, Spectrum Patrol Car, and Spectrum Pursuit Vehicle, enjoyed great popularity and long production runs between 1967 and 1979. This means that examples are still plentiful; however, as with Corgi's 1965 James Bond's Aston Martin, it is the earlier issues that are the most collectable. A good illustration of this is Dinky's model of Thunderbird 2. Issued in 1967 and measuring 5¾ inches (143mm), it was faithfully reproduced in green and contained Thunderbird 4 cast in yellow plastic. In 1974 Thunderbird 2 was reissued in a blue livery, which as every devotee of the American puppet series knows, is the wrong colour-scheme! Therefore, for reasons of accuracy, the original issue, produced between 1967 and 1973, is the more collectable and is likely to be twice as expensive.

The Corgi toy range included a comprehensive representation of media toys aimed at very young children, including Noddy's Car, Popeye's Paddle Wagon, Magic Roundabout Car, Basil Brush's Car, and Chitty-Chitty-Bang-Bang.

Collecting T.V. and media toys is a very satisfying area within the toy collecting world. Today many children's cartoon programmes appear on television at the same time as the associated media merchandize appears in the toy shops; the idea being that the toy is as important to the success of the cartoon programme as the programme is to the success of the toy. While this idea will not interest the majority of media toy collectors, it does show that programmes and associated toys are now seen as a complete marketing package, whereas previously the toy would follow a successful film or programme. It is an interest that most of us can relate to, and in many cases the collectable merchandize is still quite affordable, and easy to locate at auctions, toy fairs and swapmeets.

Above: *A lovely group of Thomas the Tank Engine die-cast toys. The Thomas the Tank Engine copyright owners are William Heinemann the publishers, and Britt Allcroft (Thomas) Ltd, 1984, 1986.*

Above: *Batman toys from the Ertl UK catalogue. Batman is a registered trademark of DC comics Inc., and, as with all media-related toys, the copyright owner is paid royalties or licensing fees by the manufacturers or distributors for every item sold.*

# ADVICE TO COLLECTORS

Whatever the toy, the rule about condition is the same—the better the condition, the nearer the toy is to looking as if it has just come out of the factory door, the more attractive it is. Such condition is usually described as 'mint'.

If a toy looks mint, but because of certain minor blemishes, scratches or chips could not fairly be described as mint, then it would be described as 'excellent'.

If a toy looks good, but has plainly been played with, although well kept and of fresh and attractive appearance, then it would be described as 'good'.

If a toy looks somewhat worn, but is nevertheless sufficiently pleasing to be collected, then it would be described as 'fair'.

Any toy in condition not good enough to be described as fair would be described as 'poor'. This description covers anything from almost collectable to totally wrecked. The normal use of poor toys is for restoration or spare parts.

All these descriptions apply to the general surface of the toy, this usually being paintwork. Any actual breakages or other major defects should be described as such. Sometimes casting faults occur in the factory. It is a matter of debate as to whether these should be viewed as defective toys, as a run-of-the-mill part of the production process, or as priceless rarities.

Naturally it is the ambition of most collectors to possess all their toys in mint condition. This means that prices for mint toys are up to three times those for fair condition. Broken or poor condition toys should be much cheaper.

The purpose of any system of description of condition is to enable collectors to buy sight unseen. Reputable dealers will offer a money-back guarantee on anything bought by post, in case the collector's idea of excellent does not match theirs. Auction houses will not always be so kind to the postal bidder. It makes sense to attend an auction and check out the auctioneer's idea of the descriptions before embarking on extensive sight-unseen bidding.

Not all dealers use the system shown here, but this one is widely recognized, and all other systems can be

Below: *A No.2 Meccano Constructor Car Kit, introduced during the 1930s. The kit would have come with accessories such as body panels, mudguards, and radiators, which were interchangeable on a common chassis. 13ins (33cms).*

Above: *Four Dinky aircraft sets in their original boxes.*

easily related to it. If confronted with the terms 'very good', 'fine' or 'slightly chipped', a telephone call will determine where on the usual scale these terms are supposed to come. Very good, for instance, might be expected to be a bit better than good but not quite excellent. An extension of the usual scale would term this 'excellent to good' or 'E-G' for short. The abbreviated scale would then run M, E, E-G, G, G-F, F, F-P, P. Where such descriptions appear in auctions, and there are more than one item in a lot, the description is likely to be an average rather than an absolute. As a rule, the more expensive the item, the more carefully it will be described.

Each method of manufacturing toys makes them prone to certain types of damage which must be looked for in assessing condition. Bisque dolls are subject to cracks and chips with rough handling. Composition tends to crack or flake at the surface. Soft toys suffer from moths, and paper toys and boxes from silverfish, insects and mice who find the glue or paper edible or useful for nesting material. Tinplate tends to rust, and lithographed tinplate is easily scratched. The paint from lead toys scratches or chips, and fragile extremities can easily bend or break. Lead is also prone to oxydize in various ways under certain condi-

tions, resulting in a brittle grey powdery appearance known to collectors as lead disease.

Die-cast toys are usually enamelled, which chips with use, the plastic parts become worn or damaged, decals or stickers damage or peel off, and thin low-friction axles bend easily. Early (and sometimes later) die-casts are prone to what collectors call metal fatigue, where impurities in the mazac alloy cause a myriad of fine cracks to appear, giving the surface a crazed look.

Plastic toys become scratched or scuffed, any paint easily flakes off, and they can appear chewed, melted, cut, gouged or twisted. The harder sorts of plastic tend to be easily snapped, and manufacturers sometimes ordered plastic mixed with chalk to make plastic figures more easily paintable, which had the same effect. The so-called unbreakable toy soldiers were often nothing of the sort.

While mint condition toys are inevitably those that are the best investment, the collector who is interested in quickly collecting a particular range of toys will not find it easy to acquire mint examples. The alternatives

are to wait until they turn up, or to buy the best condition available, and then trade up when a better condition example is found. If the collector enjoys buying and selling, this route may not even be so expensive as waiting.

For those with less money available, mint toys may be out of reach. The story of a range of toys can be told just as well with fair condition or restored items, and those collectors who concentrate on knowledge rather than condition can have just as much fun as the rest.

### BOXES

The boxes in which toys were originally sold are considered to be a completion of the toys' condition on leaving the factory. The feeling of opening the Christmas present and finding the brightly coloured box, then going inside it to the treasure within, is never forgotten from childhood.

Boxes, therefore, are highly sought-after, and the best condition for a toy is 'mint in mint box'. This means that the box is in as good a state as the toy, and since boxes are usually more easily damaged than the toys themselves, it is strictly only when the toy has been bought and the box unopened that the term should be applied. With toy soldiers it is often easy to see whether a boxed set is mint, as the string with which the soldiers are fixed in the box will not have been cut or removed. Even here, the soldiers can be restrung. This is easy to detect if the restringing has been done with the wrong string.

The condition description system above is also applied to boxes, the less good conditions describing gradual deterioration of the box. If there is any in-

terior packing material necessary to the completeness of the box or set, then its loss should be noted. If the box has a label, and this is damaged, this should also be described; likewise any additions to the box by way of childish scribble, ownership marks or repairs. A box in poor condition, however, can be assumed to have any defect without further description, as it does not add much to the value of the toy contained.

Not all toys were sold in boxes, and so cannot be 'mint and boxed'. Some were sold in sets, with a set box, some in boxes of a half dozen (usual for die-cast toys) or three dozen (usual for toy soldiers), from which the shop would sell individual pieces. These wholesale boxes with their complete complements are some of the rarest things to find, as almost inevitably they have to be discovered from a shop's unsold stock. Some toys were shipped loose, packed in any old carton.

Boxes are important for research, and often, particularly in the early part of the century, can provide useful clues as to who was distributing or repacking what. Toymakers would often sell in bulk to wholesale distributors or retailers who would pack sets under their own name. Some of today's most expensive collectors' toys come in this category, for instance the Army Service Column packed by Britains for a distributor known only by the initials C.F.E., a set that is worth about £10,000 ($16,500) in mint boxed condition.

In the post-World War II era, the changing style of packaging gives useful clues as to the order in which various colour variations were issued, and sequences of improved or changed packaging are collected as well as the toys inside. Some of the bubble packs and

## ADVICE TO COLLECTORS

*Left: Salvation Army. Britains Salvation Army Band has always been a popular subject among collectors. The figures were not generally issued in boxed sets, but were available singly from the Judd Street, London supply centre of the Salvation Army for sale to raise funds. The price for a group of figures such as these has been as high as £1,500 ($2,475), but so many have been discovered that no appreciation has taken place over the last ten years. Individual figures in good condition can be found for £50 to £100 each (c.$80 to $100). Phillips London.*

*Below: Britains set 25Z, elephant with keeper, howdah, boy and girl. Although first produced as late as 1954, this delightful set piece from the Britains' zoo is much sought-after, and an example with its original box was valued at £165 ($272) in 1990.*

### PRICES AND WHERE TO BUY

The highest prices are paid for the best condition, and boxed toys fetch between one and a half and three times the price of unboxed ones. Remembering the scale of condition, toys that are reasonably common will fetch twice as much mint as good, and twice as much good as fair. Poor or damaged toys should not fetch very much at all.

The highest prices are paid for the rarest toys, especially when it is well known how rare they are, for instance as with the rare items in the range of Jumeau dolls, Britains' toy soldiers, Dinky toys, Lehmann tin toys, Hornby trains and Corgi character merchandize. With lesser known manufacturers, rarities are not necessarily recognized as such. The major names are by far the most collected and in demand, and prices reflect this.

The highest prices are paid for the most attractive toys, for instance, Highlanders in toy soldiers, fire engines in tin toys and die-casts, steam locomotives in trains, and James Bond or the Beatles in character merchandize.

Having said this, the only price that works is one at which the buyer is prepared to buy and the seller is prepared to sell. Sometimes the two do not coincide. In toy collecting as elsewhere it is all a matter of supply and demand, and there are four major market places with their separate advantages and disadvantages.

window boxes which look so good in the shops are almost impossible to open without damaging them. These must therefore either be kept mint boxed, or a decision made to devalue them in return for the pleasure of handling the toy inside.

ELEPHANT
WITH
KEEPER
HOWDAH
AND
CHILDREN

*Above: A Carette limousine, German, c.1912, with clockwork mechanism.*

### DIRECT FROM THE PUBLIC

It is always possible to collect by asking friends and relatives, workmates and acquaintances. The extension of this is advertizing in local newspapers and searching around local antique shops, markets, charity shops, jumble sales and junk stalls. The usual experience is a great deal of frustration punctuated by the very occasional cheap purchase. Dealers are also undertaking this activity on a large scale. It saves a great deal of time to go to the dealer, but of course they will charge for the time that they have spent collecting.

### DEALERS AND SPECIALIST SHOPS

These people usually know a fair amount about the subject, and in order to buy things from them, it is as well to know as much as possible about the toys to be bought. If there are books, read them, and window-shop as much as possible before making the decision to purchase. Most shops and dealers are honest and

reputable, but their prices are not always bargains. To support themselves and their extensive expenditure in putting together a stock worth customers coming to see, they need to charge the top price that the market will bear. If plenty of funds are available, then the quickest way to a quality collection is probably by going to see the top dealers.

Dealers are also the right place to go to fill the elusive last model in a range. A top price is worth paying to get exactly the right piece. Dealers also will sell individually all the small-value things that tend to appear in huge quantities in large auction lots. Dealers also often send out postal lists, for sales of items through the mail and as a guide as to which shops are worth visiting. Dealers are a very good outlet for the quick sale of collections or surplus toys, but do not expect to receive much more than 50 per cent of the price that collectors would currently pay. Buying and selling are both a matter for negotiation.

### SWAPMEETS AND TOY SHOWS

Although swapmeets started as small gatherings of collectors wanting to exchange duplicated toys, many have grown to the stature of major toy shows, and

Above: *A group of fine early figures, representing nurses tending wounded soldiers, which fetched £2,800 ($4,620) in 1988.*

money is the usual medium of exchange. Go early, because all the best things are bought and sold as soon as they are seen. It is perfectly possible for anyone to take a stall at a swapmeet and take advantage of the usual 'first pick' available to stallholders, who are let in to set up before people without stalls.

Many shops and dealers also attend swapmeets, but are unlikely to have brought their full stock. Because selling expenses are relatively cheap, prices will tend to be cheaper than in shops, and there is often also more room for negotiation. Swapmeets are the best place to see a huge range of toys and compare prices to get a general feel of the market. There are now several swapmeets each weekend, and they occur periodically in almost every large centre of population. They are advertized in specialist toy magazines.

Swapmeets in Great Britain and the United States now boast up to 500 tables for toys, and 5,000 people attending. Toy shows are most highly developed in the United States, where a typical spread of subjects at a large show would include premiums, robots, boats, space toys and cast-iron toys as well as the subjects in

this book. The majority of British events are aimed at die-cast collectors, who outnumber all other toy collectors put together, but there are usually stalls for toy trains, toy soldiers and figures, and a few tin toys, while T.V. and media toys are to be found in all categories. Dolls and dolls' houses, however, often have specialist shows of their own, as well as appearing at certain toy shows.

## AUCTIONS

These are a method of selling goods by competitive bidding. Specialized toy sales now happen at many auction houses, from the big London firms of Sotheby's, Christie's, Phillip's and Bonham's down to the humbler provincials. Some sales are specialized by toy subjects, or sectioned, and some are designed to offer individual toys, even of quite low values, as single lots. They are also advertized in the toy collecting magazines.

Even the top-class auctions are open to all, both buying and selling, unless they are private auctions held by a club for members only. For sellers, they provide a good way of putting toys into the market and obtaining a competitive price for them direct from collectors. For buyers, they give the opportunity to buy large quantities or rare items, sometimes direct from the original person who bought them in the shop as a child. Collectors and dealers also use auctions to buy and sell. With commissions, buyers'

Above: *A very desirable Kämmer & Reinhardt Character child, with painted brown eyes and a rather passive expression, of great appeal to collectors. The modelling and quality are excellent, and it has a memorable face, which helped the doll to achieve a price of £6,000 ($9,900) at auction in 1984. Examples of such finesse never lose their value, and are excellent acquisitions.*

premiums and taxes, the difference between the selling and the buying price for an item is usually about 25 per cent.

Some collectors do not like the auction atmosphere, where the main requirements are an instant grasp of the current market price and a firm determination not to go above what can be afforded. In spite of myths to the contrary, auctioneers are tolerant of bidding mistakes. However, it is perfectly possible—and indeed often happens—that two people determined to possess a rare piece drive the price way above what might have been an expected level. Alternatively, some things will go cheap. This is what makes it fun.

Attending auctions and subscribing to their cata-

logues and sale result lists is another good way of learning how much a particular branch of toy collecting will cost.

## PRICE GUIDES
There are a number of publications with price guides. These are well worth reading, since even if prices have moved on with inflation, the comparative prices of items will be shown. Most price guides include a great deal of useful knowledge about pricing toys. The main point to make about them is that they cannot define what may be asked for a toy on any particular occasion.

## DISPLAY, STORAGE, SECURITY AND INSURANCE
Many collectors find that their collections cost so much to acquire that they have little left over to spend on display. This is a shame since the display and enjoyment of the toys is a major element of the hobby. Now that there are many more museums and displays in shops selling old toys, ideas can be taken from

---

*Left: Many firms utilized the heads manufactured by Simon & Halbig for their dolls. Interestingly, the automaton shown here, with its German head, was in fact made in France by Leopold Lombot and represents a Russian folk dancer — a truly international doll! The head is marked '1300-0 DEP S and H' and is of the standard type in modelling, not really remarkable in any way. However, it serves to create, along with the original lace costume and musical mechanism, a very collectable item. It sold for £1,300 ($2,145) at auction in 1990.*

*Below: Nodding head Mandarin. An early lead novelty figure by Britains, this figure simply nodded its head sagely. Typical of novelty figures about the turn of the century, it shows that the technology to make hollowcast toy soliders existed well before the arrival of the toys themselves. Toy soldier collectors often collect the relatively small number of other products made by Britains, out of interest in owning a complete collection of that firm's output. This figure is worth about £250 ($413). Phillips London.*

these. Scenic backgrounds are one possibility for the more realistic toys; mock shop windows, for instance, could capture the original excitement of childhood. Interesting juxtaposition of toys to make particular points about sequence or manufacturing methods enables interesting stories to be told with ease.

Display or storage should be designed to avoid the major enemy of the toy collector, damp, which causes rust, lead disease, accelerated metal fatigue and box rotting, especially in modern times with so much acid rain. This involves dry but well ventilated storage. Many collectors simply store their toys at reasonable room temperature in large cardboard boxes. The other plague is dust, so reasonably frequent dusting and moving of exhibits is recommended.

With collections that may be valuable, it is as well to give some thought to security, although the collector's best course in this is anonymity. Security measures should be as discreet as possible, and the collection should be in the house rather than in an unattended outbuilding.

Insurance is a matter of having a proper valuation acceptable to the insurance company. Most specialist auction houses or recognized experts are happy to provide this service for a fee. How much of the collection should be insured is up to the collector, but this can be expensive, and need not be done if the risk of loss can be faced.

### RESTORATION AND EMBELLISHMENT

So far, it has been assumed that the collecting of toys has been of originals, in whatever condition, that is to say, items that have not been altered after they left the toymaker. It is quite natural, however, for children to want to improve their toys, by making clothes for dolls, painting trains and soldiers, adding extra decals to racing cars or otherwise improving models. Toys in this state are for the collector no different to other toys in poor condition. The problem comes in recognizing them as being altered rather than as being original, or rare colour variations. Usually the embellishment is obvious, but sometimes it is not, and the collector should be on the lookout.

Many model collectors like to superdetail their models, and, taken as a separate hobby, this is quite acceptable. Die-cast collectors categorize models as 'code 1', unaltered; 'code 2', altered and issued with the original manufacturer's agreement; and 'code 3', without agreement. This usually applies to changes of colour, commercial livery or decals.

Restoration of toys to original condition is also acceptable, unless the intention is to pass it off as original. Many restorers and collectors mark the underside of restorations, so that in the event of these being resold in the future, they are easily distinguishable. The restoration of toys is highly time-consuming, but an interesting option for those unable to afford the prices now fetched for originals.

Right: *Modelled on a Ford of the 1950s, this battery-operated Skyliner sports car was manufactured by Namura Toys of Tokyo. 9ins (23.5cms).*

Left: *A Japanese battery-powered 'Ford-Gyron' futuristic concept car by Ichida. As the car travels about in a haphazard way, its cockpit opens and shuts. c.1955, 11ins (27.5cms) long.*

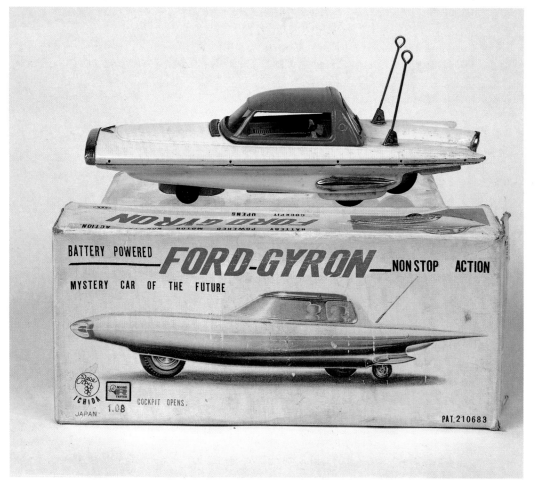

# BIBLIOGRAPHY

## GENERAL BOOKS
Gardner, Gordon, and O'Neill, Richard, *The All Colour Directory of Metal Toys* (Salamander)
O'Brien, Richard, *American Toys* (New Cavendish, 1990)
Opie, Iona and Robert, and Alderson, Brian, *The Treasures of Childhood* (Pavilion, London 1989)

## MAGAZINES
*Antique Toy World*, P.O. Box 34509, Chicago, Illinois, 60634, U.S.A.
*Collector's Showcase*, 9 issues annually, Magazines of America, U.S.A.
*Doll's House World*, Ashdown Publishing Ltd, West Sussex, England
*The International Doll's House News*, 4 issues annually, I.O.H.N. Publishing Ltd, Southampton, England
*Military Hobbies*, A. E. Morgan Publications Ltd, Stanley House, 9 West Street, Epsom, Surrey KT18 9RL, England
*Model Collector*, Link House, Dingwall Avenue, Croydon CR9 2TA, England
*Old Toy Soldier Newsletter*, 209 North Lombard, Oak Park, Illinois 60302, U.S.A.
*The Plastic Warrior*, 65 Walton Court, Woking, Surrey GU21 5EE, England
*Pupper und Spielzeug*, 8 issues annually, Gert Wohlforth Grubtl Duisburg, West Germany
*Scale Model Collector*, Argus Specialist Publications, Argus House, Boundary Way, Hemel Hempstead, Herts HP2 7ST, England
*The Teddy Bear and Friends*, Hobby House Press, Maryland, U.S.A.
*Toy Soldier Review*, 127 74th Street, North Bergen, New Jersey 07047, U.S.A.
*The U.K. Doll Directory*, an annual publication, Hugglets, Brighton, England
*The U.K. Teddy Bear Guide*, an annual directory, Hugglets, Brighton, England

## DOLLS
Cieslik, Jurgen and Marianne, *European Dolls 1800–1930* (Cassells, London 1979)
Coleman, Dorothy, Elizabeth and Evelyn, *The Collector's Book of Dolls' Clothes* (Robert Hale, London 1976)
Coleman, Dorothy, Elizabeth and Evelyn, *The Colemans on Collecting Dolls; Introduction and Doll Identification* (videotape no. 1; Concept Associates, Maryland)
Coleman, Dorothy, Elizabeth and Evelyn, *The Collector's Encyclopedia of Dolls Vols I and II* (Robert Hale, London 1968 and 1986)
Goodfellow, Caroline, *Understanding Dolls* (The Antique Collector's Club, 1986)
King, Constance Eileen, *The Collector's History of Dolls* (Robert Hale, London 1977)
Merrill, Madeleine Osbourne, *The Art of Dolls 1700–1940* (Robert Hale, London 1985)

## DOLLS' HOUSES
Earnshaw, Nora, *Collecting Dolls' Houses and Miniatures* (William Collins & Sons, London 1989)
Jacobs, Flora Gill, *Dolls' Houses in America* (Scribner, New York 1977)
King, Constance Eileen, *The Collector's History of Dolls' Houses, Doll's House Dolls and Miniatures* (Robert Hale, London 1983)
King, Constance Eileen, *Dolls and Dolls' Houses* (Hamlyn, London 1977)
Whitton, Blair, *Bliss Toys and Dolls' Houses* (Doves Publications, New York 1979)

## TIN TOYS
Bartok, Peter, *The Minic Book* (New Cavendish, 1990)
Fawdry, Marguerite, *British Tin Toys* (New Cavendish, 1990)
Gardner, Gordon and O'Neill, Richard, *Toy Cars; Transport Toys* (Salamander)
Pressland, David, *The Art of the Tin Toy* (New Cavendish)

## TEDDY BEARS
Axe, John, *The Magic of Merrythought* (Hobby House Press, Maryland, 1986)
Cieslik, Jurgen and Marianne, *Button in Ear, the Teddy Bear and his Friends* (Verlag, 1989)
Hebbs, Pam, *Collecting Teddy Bears* (William Collins & Sons, London 1988)
Hillier, Mary, *Teddy Bears: A Celebration* (Ebury Press, London 1985)

# BIBLIOGRAPHY

Mandel, Margaret Fox, *Teddy Bears and Steiff Animals* (Collector Books, Kentucky)
Schoonmaker, Patricia, *A Collector's History of the Teddy Bear* (Hobby House Press, Maryland 1981)

## TOY TRAINS
Foster, Michael, *Hornby-Dublo Trains 1938–1964* (New Cavendish)
Fuller, Roland, and Levy, Allen, *The Bassett-Lowke Story* (New Cavendish)
Graebe, Chris and Julie, *The Hornby Gauge 0 System* (New Cavendish)
Levy, Allen, *A Century of Model Trains* (New Cavendish)
McCrindell, Ron, *Toy Trains* (Salamander)

## TOY SOLDIERS AND FIGURES
Allendesalazar, J. M., *Collectionissimo de Soldades* (Editorial Everest, Spain 1979)
Baldet, Marcel, *Figurines et Soldats de Plomb* (Paris 1961)
Fontana, Dennis, *The War Toys No. 2; The Story of Lineol* (New Cavendish, 1981)
Garratt, John G., *The World Encyclopedia of Model Soldiers* (Muller, 1981) Contains both models and toys
Joplin, Norman, *British Toy Figures, 1900 to the Present* (Arms and Armour Press, 1987)
Kurtz, Henry I, and Ehrlich, Burtt R., *The Art of the Toy Soldier* (New Cavendish, 1989)
O'Brien, Richard, *Collecting Toy Soldiers* (Books Americana, 1988) Particularly good for U.S.A. makers
Opie, James, *Britains' Toy Soldiers 1893–1932* (Gollancz, London 1985)
Opie, James, *British Toy Soldiers, 1893 to the Present* (Arms and Armour Press, 1985) Includes lesser known makers
Opie, James, *Collecting Toy Soldiers* (William Collins & Sons, London 1987)
Ortmann, Erwin, *Model Tin Soldiers* (Studio Vista, London 1974)
Polaine, Reggie, *The War Toys No. 1: The Story of Hausser-Elastolin* (New Cavendish, 1979)
Roer, Hans H., *Bleisoldaten* (Callwey, 1981)
Wallis, Joe, *Regiments of all Nations* (private publication). Britain's post-World War II figures, military and civilian

## DIE-CAST TOYS
Cleemput, Marcel R. Van, *The Great Book of Corgi 1956–1983* (New Cavendish, 1989)
Greilsamer, Jacques, and Azema, Bertrand, *Catalogue of Model Cars of the World,* (Edita Lausanne, Switzerland 1967) Includes all types of cars and car kits
McGimpsey, Kevin and Orr, Stewart, *Collecting Matchbox Diecast Toys* (Major Productions, 1989)
Ramsay, John, *British Die-cast Model Toys, with Price Guide,* 3rd edition (private publication, 1988)
Richardson, Mike and Sue, *Dinky Toys and Modelled Miniatures* (New Cavendish, 1989)
Thompson, Graham, *Spot-On Diecast Models by Tri-ang* (Foulis, 1983)
Trench, Patrick, *Model Cars and Road Vehicles* (Pelham, 1983)

# INDEX

# INDEX